D0812462

The WISDOM *of* JUDAISM

Other titles in this series

The Wisdom of Hinduism, ISBN–1–85168–227–9

The Wisdom of Jesus, ISBN 1–85168–225–2

The Wisdom of Buddhism, ISBN 1–85168–226–0

The Wisdom of the Qur'an, ISBN 1–85168–224–4

The Wisdom of the Tao, ISBN 1–85168–232–5

Related titles published by Oneworld

God's BIG Book of Virtues

God's BIG Handbook for the Soul

God's BIG Instruction Book

The Oneworld Book of Prayer

Words to Comfort, Words to Heal

The WISDOM *of* JUDAISM

Compiled by Dan Cohn-Sherbok

ONEWORLD

OXFORD

THE WISDOM OF JUDAISM

Oneworld Publications
(Sales and Editorial)
185 Banbury Road
Oxford OX2 7AR
England

http://www.oneworld-publications.com

Oneworld Publications
(US Marketing Office)
160 N Washington St.
4th Floor, Boston
MA 02114
USA

A CIP record for this title is available
from the British Library

ISBN 1–85168–228–7

Cover design by Design Deluxe, Bath
Typeset by Cyclops Media Productions
Printed and bound by Graphicom Srl, Vicenza, Italy

CONTENTS

PREFACE

TODAY WE are encouraged to believe that we can find total fulfilment in the secular world. Yet for many there is a growing realization that the material world cannot offer all that is needed. As a result of this, people are turning to ancient wisdom for solutions to the problems encountered throughout their lives.

From the dawn of humankind people have struggled with the problem of how to live. For nearly four thousand years, Jews have tried to find the answers to the deepest mysteries. Beginning with the Hebrew scriptures and continuing with the outpouring of Rabbinic literature, Jewish sages have sought to resolve the most perplexing issues of human existence.

What is distinctive about Jewish wisdom is its focus on God and his action in the world. From ancient times, the Jewish nation has seen itself as God's people. According to the scriptures, God disclosed himself to them, revealed the law and brought them to the Promised Land. Through times of tribulation and suffering the Jewish people were strengthened and comforted by their faith in God. Jewish wisdom focuses on a belief in this special relationship.

Producing this brief anthology is beset with difficulties; inevitably the choice of topics as well as sources quoted is highly selective. Thus, there is no aim to provide an exhaustive account of Jewish wisdom. Nonetheless, the sayings contained in this volume constitute a glimpse into the treasurehouse of Jewish literature.

It is my hope that this collection will inspire the modern reader, just as the wisdom of Judaism encouraged people in previous ages. Jewish wisdom is not just for Jews; it is for anyone who seeks spiritual enlightenment, and the dilemmas it confronts are universal. The extracts in this book range from those that seek to help people to solve everyday problems involving work, family and public life; to those that try to answer more spiritual questions relating to the nature of God and the meaning of life itself.

DAN COHN-SHERBOK

By air mail
Par avion

IBRS/CCRI NUMBER:
PHQ/D/1154/OX

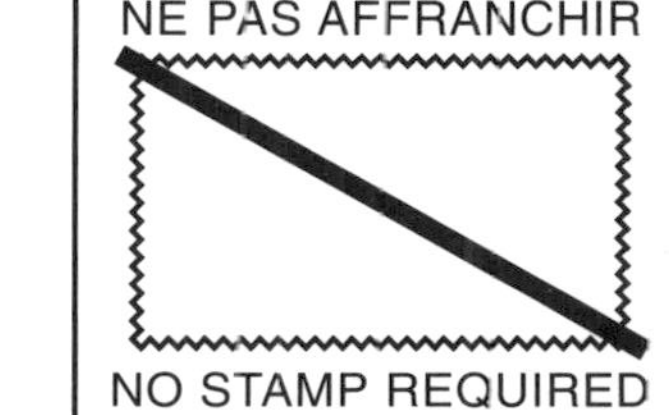

REPONSE PAYEE
GRANDE-BRETAGNE

Oneworld Publications
185 Banbury Road
OXFORD
GREAT BRITAIN
OX2 7BR

GOD

THE NATURE OF GOD

TORAH AND philosophy are in flagrant contradiction when they attempt to describe the divine essence. For the philosophers, the incorporeal God is in no way capable of alteration. The Torah, on the contrary, narrates God's movements, his feelings.

ABRAHAM IBN DAUD

HOW EXCELLENT is thy loving kindness, O God! therefore the children of men put their trust under the shadow of thy wings. For with thee is the fountain of life: in thy light shall we see light.

Psalm 36:7, 9

A PHILOSOPHER without religion is like a man standing in the desert without any society.

ISAAC PULGAR

LET NOT the wise man glory in his wisdom, let not the mighty man glory in his might, let not the rich man glory in his riches. But let him glory in this, that he understands and knows me, that I am the Lord who practises steadfast love, justice and righteousness in the earth.

MOSES MAIMONIDES

THE SUN shall be no more thy light by day; neither for brightness shall the moon give light unto thee: but the Lord shall be unto thee an everlasting light, and thy God thy glory.

Isaiah 60:19

THE LORD, the Lord God, merciful and gracious, long-suffering, and abundant in goodness and truth. Keeping mercy for thousands, forgiving iniquity and transgression and sin, and that will by no means clear the guilty; visiting the iniquity of the fathers upon the children, unto the third and to the fourth generation.

Exodus 34:6–7

GOD, WHOM shall I compare to thee,
When thou to none canst likened be?
Under what image shall I dare
To picture thee, when everywhere
All nature's forms thine impress bear?

JUDAH HALEVI

IN WHOSE hand is the soul of every living thing, and the breath of mankind.

Job 12:10

A KING usually has dukes and regents who share the burdens of his office and also share in the deference he receives, but this is not so with God. God has no duke nor governor nor lieutenant. He shares his work with no one; he does it all by himself. No one else shares the burdens with him; he bears them by himself. Therefore he alone is to be worshipped.

Midrash Psalms

GOD SAID to Israel: Because you have seen so many manifestations of me, this does not mean that there are many gods. It is always the same God. I am the Lord your God.

Pesikta Kahana

FOR I am the Lord your God: ye shall therefore sanctify yourselves, and ye shall be holy: for I am holy.

Leviticus 11:44

I SAW also the Lord sitting upon a throne, high and lifted up, and his train filled the temple. Above it stood the seraphims: each one had six wings; with twain he covered his face, and with twain he covered his feet, and with twain he did fly. And one cried unto the other, and said, Holy, holy, holy, is the Lord of hosts: the whole earth is full of his glory.

Isaiah 6:1–3

I KNEW that thou art a gracious God, and merciful, slow to anger, and of great kindness.

Jonah 4:2

WHOM HAVE I in heaven but thee? and there is none upon earth that I desire beside thee.

Psalm 73:25

AND IT shall come to pass in the last days, that the mountain of the Lord's house shall be established in the top of the mountains, and shall be exalted above the hills; and all nations shall flow unto it. And many people shall go and say, Come ye, and let us go up to the mountain of the Lord, to the house of the God of Jacob; and he will teach of his ways, and we will walk in his paths: for out of Zion shall go forth the law, and the word of the Lord from Jerusalem.

Isaiah 2:2–3

WHILE GOD'S face is above, his heart is below.

Song of Songs Rabbah

WE HOLD that Judaism presents the highest conception of the God-idea as taught in our holy scriptures and developed and spiritualized by the Jewish teachers in accordance with the moral and philosophical progress of their respective ages.

Pittsburgh Platform

THE DAY of the Lord is near in the valley of decision. The sun and the moon shall be darkened, and the stars shall withdraw their shining. The Lord also shall roar out of Zion, and utter his voice from Jerusalem; and the heavens and the earth shall shake: but the Lord will be the hope of his people, and the strength of the children of Israel.

Joel 3:14–16

THE LORD is my light and my salvation: whom shall I fear?

Psalm 27:1

OMNIPOTENCE

NOT AS man's capacity is the capacity of God. A man cannot say two words at the same time. But God proclaimed the Ten Commandments at one and the same moment. A man cannot hearken to two people who cry before him together. But God can hearken to all the inhabitants of the world if they cry simultaneously before him. As it is said, 'O thou that hearest prayer, unto thee does all flesh come.' (Psalm 65: 2)

Mekhilta

HE (GOD) created evil by creating the possibility for evil; he made peace by creating the possibility for it. He had to create the possibility for evil, if he was to create the possibility for its opposite, peace, goodness, love ... God's very mercy and forbearance, his very love for man, necessitates the abandonment of some men to a fate they may well experience as indifferent to justice and human suffering.

ELIEZER BERKOVITS

THE WAYS of God are not as the ways of man. A human king does not both wage war and teach children. But God is not like this. One day he wages war, as it is said, 'The Lord is a man of war' (*Exodus 15: 3*). The next day, at the giving of the Law, he comes down to teach the Law to his children.

Exodus Rabbah

'GOD SPOKE all these things,' (*Exodus 20: 1*). God can do everything at once. He kills and makes alive at one and the same time. He strikes and heals. He answers the prayer of the woman in travail, of those who are upon the sea, or in the desert, or who are bound in prison. He hears them all at once, whether they are in the east, west, north or south. He hearkens to all at once.

Exodus Rabbah

OMNIPRESENCE

'MY LOVE is like a gazelle.' (Song of Songs 2: 9.) As the gazelle leaps from place to place, and from fence to fence, and from tree to tree, so God jumps and leaps from synagogue to synagogue to bless the children of Israel.

Numbers Rabbah

AS GOD fills the whole world, so also the soul fills the whole body. As God sees, yet cannot be seen, so also the soul sees but cannot be seen. As God nourishes the whole world, so also the soul nourishes the whole body. As God is pure, so also is the soul pure. As God dwells in the inmost part of the universe, so also the soul dwells in the inmost part of the body.

Talmud

WHEN THREE sit and judge, the Divine Presence is in their midst.

Talmud

GOD SAYS, 'Who has ever come into a synagogue, and has not found my glory there?' 'And not only that,' said Rabbi Aibu, 'but if you are in a synagogue, God stands by you' (*Psalm 82*).

Deuteronomy Rabbah

RABBI ANNANIEL said: God says, 'If I choose, my glory fills the whole world, as it is said, "Do I not fill heaven and earth?" (*Jeremiah 23: 24*). And if I choose, I speak with Job out of the whirlwind (*Job 38: 1*) or with Moses from the thorn bush.'

Exodus Rabbah

IT IS written: 'And Moses was not able to enter into the tent of meeting, because the glory of the Lord filled the sanctuary' (*Exodus 40: 35*). Rabbi Joshua of Sikhnin said in the name of Rabbi Levi: The matter is like a cave near the sea shore: the tide rises, and the cave fills with water. But the sea is no less full. So the sanctuary and the tent of meeting were filled with the radiance of the Divine Presence, but the world was no less filled with God's glory.

Numbers Rabbah

A HEATHEN asked Rabbi Joshua ben Karha: 'Why did God speak to Moses from the thorn bush?' Rabbi Joshua replied: 'If he had spoken from a carob tree or from a sycamore, you would have asked me the same question. So as not to dismiss you without an answer, God spoke from the thorn bush to teach you that there is no place where the Divine Presence is absent, not even in a thorn bush.'

Exodus Rabbah

WHITHER SHALL I go from thy spirit? or whither shall I flee from thy presence?

If I ascend up into heaven, thou art there: if I make my bed in hell, behold thou art there.

If I take the wings of the morning and dwell in the uttermost parts of the sea:

Even there shall thy hand lead me, and my right hand shall hold me.

If I say, Surely the darkness shall cover me; even the night shall be light about me.

Yea, the darkness hideth not from thee; but the night shineth as the day.

Psalm 139:7–12

GOD IS far off since he is in the deepest heavens, but he is also near … When a man goes into a synagogue and stands behind a column and prays in a whisper, God still hears his prayer. It is the same with all his creatures. Can there be a closer God than this? He is as close to his creatures as the ear is to the mouth.

Talmud

RABBI JUDAH ben Simon said: An idol is near and far, but God is far and near. This is because an idol worshipper makes an idol and puts it in his house. Thus the idol is near, but however much he cries to the idol, it will not answer. Therefore it is far. But God is far and near. This is because the journey from here to Heaven takes five hundred years. So God is far. But if a man prays and meditates in his heart, then God answers prayers and is near.

Midrash Deuteronomy

'UNTO THEE do I lift up my eyes. O thou that sittest in the heavens' (*Psalm 123:1*). This implies that when I do not lift up my eyes, thou wouldst not be sitting in the heavens.

Midrash Psalms

A PAGAN woman said to R. Jose: 'My god is greater than your god. When your god appeared to Moses in the thorn bush, he hid his face. But when he saw my god, the snake, he fled (*Exodus 4:3*). R. Jose replied: 'When our God appeared to Moses in the thorn bush, there was no place where he could have fled. Where could he have gone? To heaven? To sea? To land? For our God declares: "Do I not fill heaven and earth?" However, from your god, the snake, a man has only to run a few steps to save himself.'

Exodus Rabbah

LORD WHERE shall I find you?
High and hidden is your place.
And where shall I not find you?
The world is full of your glory.

I have sought your nearness.
With all my heart I called you
And going out to meet you
I found you coming to meet me.

JUDAH HALEVI

WHERE I wander – you!
Where I ponder – you!
Only you, you again, always you!
You! You! You!
When I am gladdened – you!
When I am saddened – you!
Only you, you again, always you!
You! You! You!
Sky is you! Earth is you!
You above! You below!
In every trend, at every end,
Only you, you again, always you!
You! You! You!

LEVI YITZCHAK OF BERDITCHEV

WHERE IS the dwelling of God? This is the question with which the Rabbi of Kotzk surprised a number of learned men who happened to be visiting him. They laughed at him: 'What a thing to ask! Is not the whole world full of his glory?' Then he answered his own question: 'God dwells wherever man lets him in.'

MARTIN BUBER

WITHOUT GOD, life is a lonely darkness, even for the man who is in the midst of many other men and even for the man who enjoys pleasures and power.

LEO BAECK

AND HE said, Go forth, and stand upon the mount before the Lord. And, behold, the Lord passed by, and a great and strong wind rent the mountains, and brake in pieces the rocks before the Lord; but the Lord was not in the wind: and after the wind was an earthquake; but the Lord was not in the earthquake: And after the earthquake a fire; but the Lord was not in the fire: and after the fire a still small voice.

1 Kings 19:11–12

OMNISCIENCE

THE LORD seeth not as man seeth; for man looketh on the outward appearance, but the Lord looketh on the heart.

I Samuel 16:7

BEFORE A thought is framed in a man's heart, it is known already to God. Even before a person is fully formed, his thought is manifest to God.

Genesis Rabbah

I BEFORE thy greatness
Stand and am afraid:
All my secret thoughts thine eye beholdeth
Deep within my bosom laid.

SOLOMON IBN GABIROL

ALL IS forseen, yet freedom of choice is granted. By grace is the universe judged, yet all is according to the amount of the work.

Sayings of the Fathers

TRULY YOU are the one who judges and tests, probes and bears witness. You record and seal, count and measure. You remember all that is forgotten. You open the Book of Memory; it speaks for itself, for everyone has signed it by their life.

High Holyday Prayer

YOURS ARE the secrets that no mind or thought can encompass.

SOLOMON IBN GABIROL

NAMES OF GOD

THE 50TH Psalm begins: '*El, Elohim, Adonai* has spoken'. The heretics asked R. Simlai: 'Why does it say, "*El, Elohim, Adonai* has spoken?"'He replied: 'It does not say: "They spoke and they called." Rather, the verb is in the singular: "He spoke, and he called." ' His disciples then said to him: 'These men you have driven away with a broken weed (a poor argument). How would you answer us?' He said: 'All three names are in fact only one name, even as one man can be called workman, builder, architect.' 'But,' they asked, 'why then does the Psalmist mention the name of God three times?' He replied: 'To teach you that God created the world with three names, corresponding to the three good attributes by which the world was created, namely, wisdom, understanding and knowledge. As it says: "The Lord by wisdom has founded the earth, by understanding has he established the heavens, by his knowledge the depths were broken up." '

Midrash Psalms

DIVINE MANIFESTATIONS

GOD SAID to Israel, 'Because you have seen me in many likenesses, you might think there are many gods. But it is always the same God. I am the Lord your God.' Rabbi Levi said: 'God appeared to them like a mirror in which many faces can be reflected. A thousand people look at it – it looks at all of them. So when God spoke to the Israelites each one thought that God spoke individually to him. Thus it states: "I am the Lord thy God", rather than collectively: "I am the Lord your God." 'The word of God', said R. Jose b. Hanina, 'spoke with each man according to his power. You should not marvel at this for the manna tasted different to each person: to children, the young and the old, according to their power. If the manna tasted different according to the power of each, how much more the word.'

Pesikta de-Rav Kahana

REVELATION

AND HE came to a certain place, and stayed there that night, because the sun had set. Taking one of the stones of the place, he put it under his head and lay down in that place to sleep. And he dreamed that there was a ladder set up on the earth, and the top of it reaching to heaven; and behold, the angels of God were ascending and descending on it! And behold the Lord stood above it and said, 'I am the Lord, the God of Abraham your father and the God of Isaac: the Land on which you lie I will give to you and your descendants.'

Genesis 28:11–13

AND JACOB was left alone; and a man wrestled with him until the breaking of the day. When the man saw that he did not prevail against Jacob, he touched the hollow of his thigh; and Jacob's thigh was put out of joint as he wrestled with him. Then he said, 'Let me go, for the day is breaking.' But Jacob said, 'I will not let you go, unless you bless me.' And he said to him, 'What is your name?' And he said, 'Jacob.' Then he said, 'Your name shall no more be called Jacob, but Israel for you have striven with God and with men, and have prevailed.'

Genesis 32:24–28

AND THE angel of the Lord appeared to him in a flame of fire out of the midst of a bush; and he looked, and lo, the bush was burning, yet it was not consumed. And Moses said, 'I will turn aside and see this great sight, why the bush is not burnt.' When the Lord saw that he turned aside to see, God called to him out of the bush, 'Moses, Moses!' And he said, 'Here am I.' Then he said, 'Do not come near; put your shoes from your feet for the place on which you are standing is holy ground.'

Exodus 3:2–5

CREATION

WHEN GOD gave the Law, no bird sang or flew; no ox bellowed. The angels did not fly. The Seraphim ceased saying: 'Holy, holy.' The sea was calm. No creature spoke. The world was silent and still, and the divine voice said: 'I am the Lord thy God.' If you wonder at this, think of Elijah. When he went to Mount Carmel and summoned all the priests of Baal and said to them, 'Cry aloud, for he is God.' God caused the world to be still, and those above and below were silent. The world was, as it were, empty and void as if no creature existed, as it says, 'There was no voice nor any answer' (I Kings 18:29). For if anyone had spoken, the priests would have said: 'Baal has answered us'. Therefore, at Sinai God made the whole world silent so that all creatures would know that there is no god beside him. So he said, 'I am the Lord, thy God', and soon, too, in the days to come, he will say, 'I, and I alone, am he that comforts you.' (*Isaiah 51:12*)

Exodus Rabbah

WHO IS this that darkeneth counsel by words without knowledge?
Gird up now thy loins like a man; for I will demand of thee, and answer thou me.
Where wast thou when I laid the foundations of the earth? declare, if thou hast understanding.
Who hath laid the measures thereof, if thou knowest? or who hath stretched the line upon it?
Whereupon are the foundations thereof fastened? or who laid the corner stone thereof.

Job 38:2–6

WHO HATH made man's mouth? or who maketh the dumb, or deaf, or the seeing, or the blind? have not I the Lord?

Exodus 4:11

AMONG ALL the things which God created in his universe, he created nothing that is useless. He created the snail as a cure for a wound, the fly as a cure for the sting of the wasp, the gnat as a cure for the bite of the serpent, the serpent as a cure for a sore, and the spider as a cure for the sting of a scorpion.

Talmud

THE EARTH is the Lord's, and the fulness thereof; the world and they that dwell therein. For he hath founded it upon the seas, and established it upon the floods. Who shall ascend into the hill of the Lord? or who shall stand in his holy place? He that hath clean hands, and a pure heart; who hath not lifted up his soul unto vanity, nor sworn deceitfully.

Psalm 24:1–4

THE SCHOOLS of Hillel and Shammai disputed two and a half years whether it would have been better if man had or had not been created. Eventually they agreed that it would have been better if he had not been created. But since he had been created, let him investigate his past actions, and let him examine what he is about to do.

Talmud

THE HEAVENS declare the glory of God; and the firmament sheweth his handywork.

Psalm 19:1

ONE GENERATION passeth away, and another generation cometh: but the earth abideth for ever.

Ecclesiastes 1:4

YEA, THE darkness hideth not from thee; but the night shineth as the day: the darkness and the light are both alike to thee. For thou hast possessed my reins; thou hast covered me in my mother's womb. I will praise thee; for I am fearfully and wonderfully made: marvellous are thy works; and that my soul knoweth right well. My substance was not hid from thee, when I was made in secret, and curiously wrought in the lowest parts of the earth.

Psalm 139:12–15

WHEN I consider thy heavens, the work of thy fingers, the moon and the stars, which thou hast ordained; What is man, that thou art mindful if him? and the son of man, that thou visitest him. For thou hast made him a little lower than the angels, and hast crowned him with glory and honour. Thou madest him to have dominion over the works of thy hands; thou hast put all things under his feet.

Psalm 8:3–6

THE JEWISH PEOPLE

ISRAEL

RABBI AZARIAH said in the name of Rabbi Judah ben Simon: 'When the Israelites do God's will, they add to the power of God on high. But when the Israelites do not do God's will, they as it were, weaken the great power of God on high.'

Lamentations Rabbah

WAS ISRAEL created for the sake of the Law, or the Law for the sake of Israel? Surely the Law for the sake of Israel. Now if the Law which was created for the sake of Israel will endure forever, how much more will Israel which was created by the merit of the Law.

Ecclesiastes Rabbah

ONE THING is to me certain, high above any doubt: the movement will continue. I know not when I shall die, but Zionism will never die.

THEODOR HERZL

GOD SAID to Israel, 'Make me a dwelling (*Exodus 25:8*), for I desire to dwell amid my sons.' When the ministering angels heard this, they said to God, 'Why will you abandon the creatures above, and descend to those below? It is your glory that you should be in heaven, "O Lord our God, who hast set thy majesty in the heavens." ' (*Psalm 8:1*). But God said, 'See how greatly I love the creatures below that I shall descend and dwell beneath the goats' hair.' Hence it says: 'Make curtains of goats' hair for the Tabernacle.' (*Exodus 26:7*)

Tanhuma

A MAN said to me, 'My master, why do the gentiles enjoy this world?' I replied, 'My son, this is their reward because God separated Israel from among them. It is like a king who found that one man, out of a large family, did his will. The king sent gifts to all the members of the family for the sake of that single man who did the king's will. So it is with the gentiles. They enjoy this world as a reward that God separated Israel from among them.'

Tanna de be Eliyyahu

IT IS the custom among men when they appear before a court of justice to put on black clothes, and to let the beard grow long because of the uncertainty of the issue. Israelites do not act so. On the day when the judgment opens, they are clad in white and shave their beards; they eat and drink and rejoice in the conviction that God will do wonders for them.

Talmud

A HERETIC said to Rabbi Hanina: 'Now that the Temple is destroyed, and you cannot cleanse yourselves from your uncleanness, you are defiled, and God no longer dwells among you.' He replied: 'It is written, "He dwells among them in the mist of their uncleanness".'

Talmud

RABBI LEVI said: 'As the bee gathers everything which it gathers for its owner, so whatever the Israelites gather of commandents and good works, they gather for their Father in Heaven.'

Deuteronomy Rabbah

RABBI JOSHUA Ben Levi said: 'Not even an iron wall can separate Israel from their Father in Heaven.'

Talmud

AND THEY shall stumble, one man by his brother (*Leviticus 26:37*). This means that one man will stumble because of the sin of his brother. Hence learn that every Israelite is surety for every other.

Sifra

GOD SAYS: 'I testify by heaven and earth that I sit and hope for Israel more than a father for his son or than a mother for her daughter, if only they would repent, so that my words could be fulfilled.'

Tanna de be Eliyyahu

AS THE lily dies only with its scent, so Israel will not die so long as it executes the commands and does good deeds.

Song of Songs Rabbah

HADRIAN SAID to Rabbi Joshua: 'Great indeed must be the lamb, Israel, that can exist among seventy wolves.' He replied: 'Great is the shepherd who rescues and protects her.'

Tanhuma

'MANY WATERS cannot quench love' (*Song of Songs 8:7*). If the idolatrous nations of the world united to destroy the love between God and Israel, they would not be able to do so.

Exodus Rabbah

IF ONLY I could roam through those places where God was revealed to your prophets and heralds. Who will give me wings so that I may wander far away? I would carry the pieces of my broken heart over the rugged mountains. I would bow down my face on your ground; I would love your stones.

JUDAH HALEVI

ALL ISRAELITES are mutually accountable for each other. In a boat at sea one of the men began to bore a hole in the bottom of the boat. On being criticized, he answered: 'I am only boring under my own seat.' 'Yes,' replied the others, 'but when the sea rushes in we shall all be drowned with you.' So it is with Israel.

Talmud

BEYOND THE howling desert with its sand
There waits beneath his stars the Promised Land.

HAYIM NAHMAN BIALIK

EXILE

RABBI HENOCH of Alexander once said: The real exile of Israel in Egypt was that they learned to endure it.

Hasidic Tale

EVEN THOUGH Israel be in exile among the nations, if they occupy themselves with Torah, it is though they were not exiled.

Tanna de be Eliyyahu

WHEN YOU leave Egypt, any Egypt, do not stop to think: 'But how will I earn a living out there?' One who stops to make provision for the way will never get out of Egypt.

NAHMAN OF BRATSLAV

JUDAISM

WAS JUDAISM ever 'in accordance with the times'? Did Judaism ever correspond with the views of dominant contemporaries? Was it ever convenient to be a Jew or a Jewess?

SAMSON RAPHAEL HIRSCH

HEBREW

THE HEBREW language is the great depository of all that is best in the soul-life of the congregation of Israel. Without it we will become severed from the great tree which is life to those who cling to it.

SOLOMON SCHECHTER

CONVERTS

DEARER TO God is the convert who has come of his own accord than all the crowds of Israelites who stood before Mount Sinai.

Tanhuma

IF A person wishes to become a convert, but says, 'I am too old. At this time I cannot become a convert', let him learn from Abraham, who when he was ninety-nine years old, entered God's covenant.

Tanhuma

GOD COMMANDED the Israelites to do good to converts and to treat them with gentleness.

Sifre Numbers

THE RABBIS say: Now if someone comes and wants to be a convert, say to him: 'Why do you want to be a convert. Don't you know that the Israelites are harried, hounded, persecuted and harassed and that they suffer many troubles?' If he replies: 'I know that and I am not worthy', then they receive him without further argument.

Talmud

COVENANT

I DO set my bow in the cloud, and it shall be for a token of a covenant between me and the earth. And it shall come to pass, when I bring a cloud over the earth, that the bow shall be seen in the cloud: And I will remember my covenant which is between me and you and every living creature of all flesh; and the waters shall no more become a flood to destroy all flesh.

Genesis 9:13–15

NOW THE Lord said to Abram, 'Go from your country and your kindred and your father's house to the land that I will show you. And I will make of you a great nation, and make your name great, so that you will be a blessing. I will bless those who bless you, and him who curses you I will curse; and through you all the families of the earth shall bless themselves.'

Genesis 12:1–3

ON SEEING a rainbow, one recites the blessing: Blessed are you, Lord our God, king of the universe, who remembers his covenant, is faithful to it, and keeps his promise.

Jewish Prayer Book

WHEN THEY came to the place of which God had told him, Abraham built an altar there, and laid the wood in order, and bound Isaac his son, and laid him on the altar, upon the wood. Then Abraham put forth his hand and took the knife to slay his son. But the angel of the Lord called to him from heaven, and he said, 'Abraham, Abraham!' And he said, 'Here am I.' He said, 'Do not lay your hand on the lad or do anything to him; for now I know that you fear God, seeing you have not withheld your son, your only son, from me.'

Genesis 22:9–13

PREJUDICE

I REMEMBER when I used to come home from the *cheder* (Hebrew School), bleeding and crying from the wounds inflicted upon me by the Christian boys, my father used to say, 'My child, we are in *Golus* (exile), and we must submit to God's will.' And he made me understand that this is only a passing stage in history, as we Jews belong to eternity, when God will comfort his people. Thus the pain was only physical; but my real suffering began later in life, when I emigrated from Roumania to so-called civilized countries, and found there what I might call the Higher Anti-Semitism, which burns the soul though it leaves the body unhurt.

SOLOMON SCHECHTER

THE JEWS are not hated because they have evil qualities; evil qualities are sought for in them because they are hated.

MAX NORDEAU

NOT ONE man alone has risen up against us to destroy us, but in every generation there rise up against us those who seek to destroy us.

Passover Haggadah

RESPONSIBILITY

DON'T SHELTER yourself in any course of action by the idea that 'it is my affair.' It is your affair, but it is also mine and the community's. Nor can we neglect the world beyond. A fierce light beats upon the Jew. It is a grave responsibility this – to be a Jew; and you can't escape from it, even if you choose to ignore it.

C.G. MONTEFIORE

SYNAGOGUE

THE SYNAGOGUE is the sanctuary of Israel. It was born out of Israel's longing for the living God. It has been to Israel throughout his endless wanderings a visible token of the presence of God in the midst of the people. It has shed a beauty which is the beauty of holiness and has ever stood on the high places as the champion of justice and brotherhood and peace. It is Israel's sublime gift to the world.

Union Prayerbook

JEWISH LAW

TORAH

ALL THE nations of the world were invited to receive the Torah ... They were asked, but they did not accept it ... But when he came to Israel, they all declared: 'All that the Lord has commanded, we will do, and we will be obedient.' *(Exodus 24:7)*

Mekhilta

ADOPT THE customs and constitution of the country in which you live, but also be careful to follow the religion of your fathers. As well as you can, you must carry both burdens. It is not easy because, on the one hand, people make it hard for you to carry the burden of civil life because of your faithfulness to your religion and, on the other hand, the climate of the times makes keeping religious law harder than it need be in some respects. Nevertheless, you must try. Stand fast in the place you have been allocated by Providence and submit to everything that happens to you as you were commanded long ago by your law giver.

MOSES MENDELSSOHN

THROUGH THE Torah God created the world, the Torah was his helper and his tool. With its aid, he set boundaries to the deep, ordered the orbits of the sun and the moon and formed all of nature. Without the Torah, the world would disappear.

Tanhuma

THE WORDS of the Torah are like fire. Both were given from heaven; both are eternal. If a person draws near fire, he derives benefit. If he keeps far away, he freezes. Similarly with the words of Torah. If one toils in them, they are life to him. But if he separates from them, they kill him.

Sifre Deuteronomy

SCRIPTURE MUST be interpreted according to its plain, natural sense, each word according to the context. Traditional exposition, however, may also be taken to heart, as it is said: 'Is not my word like as fire?' – consisting of many sparks – 'and like a hammer that breaketh the rock in pieces?' – and therefore capable of various explanations.

RASHI

RABBI BANNA'AH used to say: 'If one studies the Torah for its own sake, it becomes an elixir of life. But if one studies the Torah not for its own sake, it becomes a deadly poison.'

Talmud

WHOEVER ACKNOWLEDGES idols, repudiates the whole Torah. But whoever repudiates idolatry is as though he accepted the whole Torah.

Sifre Deuteronomy

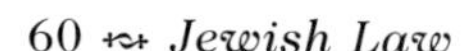

SABBATH

RABBI HIYYA ben Abba said: 'When the mother of Simeon ben Yohai talked too much on the Sabbath, he would say to her, "Mother, it is Sabbath", and she would stop.'

Pesikta Rabbati

FAR MORE than Israel has kept the Sabbath, it is the Sabbath that has kept Israel.

AHAD HA'AM

LEGAL STATUTES

FOR THIS commandment which I command thee this day, it is not hidden from thee, neither is it far off. It is not in heaven, that thou shouldest say, Who shall go up for us to heaven, and bring it unto us, that we may hear it, and do it? Neither is it beyond the sea, that thou shouldest say, Who shall go over the sea for us, and bring it unto us, that we may hear it, and do it? But the word is very nigh unto thee, in thy mouth, and in thy heart, that thou mayest do it.

Deuteronomy 30:11–14

WITH EVERLASTING love you have loved the house of Israel, your people; a Law and commandments, statutes and judgements have you taught us. Therefore, O Lord our God, when we lie down and when we rise up we will meditate on your statutes. Yea, we will rejoice in the words of your Law and in your commandments for ever; for they are our life and the length of our days.

Jewish Prayer Book

RABBI ZADOK said, 'Do not make (the Law) a crown wherewith to aggrandise yourself, nor a spade wherewith to dig.'

Sayings of the Fathers

WITH REGARD to the commandment of the fringes (*Numbers 15:39*) it says, 'You shall see it.' So when the Israelites look at the fringes, it should seem to them as though the Divine Presence were resting on them.

Tanhuma

RABA SAID: 'As for him who does not fulfil the Torah for its own sake, it would have been better if he had not been created.'

Talmud

IF YOU become slack about one commandment, you will end by becoming slack about another. If you despise one, you will end up by despising another.

Derek Erez Zuta

WHEN LAW came into the world, freedom came into the world.

Genesis Rabbah

RAB SAID: 'The commandments were given to Israel only so that men should be purified through them. For what can it matter to God whether a beast is slain at the throat or at the neck?

Genesis Rabbah

RABA SAID: 'For those who make a right use of the Law, it is a drug for life. For those who make a wrong use, it is a drug for death.'

Talmud

SIMON HIS son said, 'I was brought up all my life amongst the sages, and I have found nothing so essentially good as silence. It is not the study (of the Law) which is of fundamental importance, but the practice (of it). Whosoever is profuse of words occasions sin.

Sayings of the Fathers

RABBI ELISHA ben Abuyah said: 'If a man causes another to do a commandment, Scripture regards him as if he had done it himself.'

Avot de-Rabbi Nathan

IT IS like a king who said to his wife, 'Deck yourself with all your ornaments that you may be acceptable to me.' Thus God says to Israel: 'Be distinguished by the commandments so that you may be acceptable to me.' As it says: 'Fair art thou, my beloved, when thou art acceptable to me.'

Sifre Deuteronomy

TEACH THE Law for free, and take no fee for it. For the words of the Law no fee must be taken since God gave the Law for free. Whoever takes a fee for the Law destroys the world.

Derek Erez Zuta

IF IT were not for my Law which you accepted, I should not recognize you, and should not regard you more than any of the idolatrous nations of the world.

Exodus Rabbah

BEN AZZAI said: 'If a man humiliates himself for the Law, eats dry dates, wears dirty clothes, and sits keeping guard at the doors of the wise, every passer-by will think him a fool. But at the end you will find that all the Law is within him.'

Avot de-Rabbi Nathan

RABBI JONATHAN said, 'Whoever fulfils the Law in poverty shall in the end fulfil it in wealth. But whoever discards the Law in wealth shall ultimately neglect it in poverty.'

Sayings of the Fathers

HE USED to say, 'The more flesh, the more worms. The more possessions, the more anxiety. The more wives, the more witchcraft. The more maidservants, the more lasciviousness. The more menservants, the more robbery. The more (study of) the Law, the more life; the more schooling, the more wisdom. The more counsel, the more understanding. The more charity, the more peace. Whoever has gained a good name has acquired (a gain) for himself. One who has acquired for himself words of the Law has gained for himself life in the world to come.'

Sayings of the Fathers

חג המצות
באורך נראה אור
להדליק נר של יום טוב
פסח
והגדת לבנך ביום ההוא
מצרים
שיר השירים

COMMANDMENTS

HE WHO loves the commandments is never satiated with them.

Deuteronomy Rabbah

IT SAYS in the Psalms, 'Happy is the man who fears the Lord and delights greatly in his commandments.' Rabbi Elazar said: "In his commandments, but not in the reward of his commandments."

Talmud

THE STATUTES of the Lord are right, rejoicing the heart: the commandment of the Lord is pure, enlightening the eyes. The fear of the Lord is clean, enduring for ever: the judgments of the Lord are true and righteous altogether. More to be desired are they than gold, yea, than much fine gold: sweeter also than honey and the honeycomb.

Psalm 19:8–10

BELOVED ARE the Israelites for God has encompassed them with commandments: phylacteries on the head and arm, fringes on their garments, *mezuzot* on their doors.

Talmud

HE WHO violates a light command will ultimately violate a heavy one. He who violates, 'Love thy neighbour as thyself,' will ultimately violate, 'Thou shalt not hate thy brother in thy heart, and thou shalt not take vengeance nor bear any grudge.' And even, 'He shall live with thee' (*Leviticus 25:35*), till at the end he will come to shedding blood.

Sifre Deuteronomy

MY SON, keep my words, and lay up my commandments with thee. Keep my commandments and live; and my law as the apple of thine eye. Bind them upon thy fingers, write them upon the table of thine heart.

Proverbs 7:1–3

THOU SHALT love the Lord, thy God with all thine heart, and with all thy soul, and with all thy might. And these words which I command thee this day, shall be in thine heart: And thou shalt teach them diligently unto thy children, and shalt talk of them when thou sittest in thine house, and when thou walkest by the way, and when thou liest down, and when thou risest up. And thou shalt bind them for a sign upon thine hand, and they shall be as frontlets between thine eyes. And thou shalt write them upon the posts of thy house, and on thy gates.

Deuteronomy 6:5–9

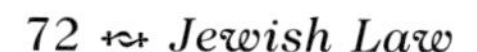

JUSTICE

TO EVERY judge who judges justly, even for an hour, Scripture reckons it as if he had been a partner with God in creation.

Talmud

HE USED to say, 'Judge not alone, for no one may judge alone save One.'

Sayings of the Fathers

GOD DOES not withold the due reward of any of his creatures, even of the mouse which preserved its family and mated with its kind – not like the men of the generation of the flood who were promiscuous.

Tanhuma

HE WHO judges justly is a co-worker with God.

Exodus Rabbah

YE SHALL have one manner of law, as well for the stranger, as for one of your own country: for I am the Lord your God.

Leviticus 24:22

HE WHO judges his neighbour favourably will himself be judged favourably by God.

Talmud

MY LAST word is that each case must be judged on its own merits, for the correct application of the Law depends on the virtuous intention of the heart. Our Torah, which is true, upholds truth above every other consideration so the judge must make up his mind in accordance with the truth.

SOLOMON IBN ADRET

THESE ARE the things that ye shall do; Speak ye every man the truth to his neighbour; execute the judgment of truth and peace in your gates. And let none of you imagine evil in your hearts against his neighbour.

Zechariah 8:16–17

WHEN A person appears before the Throne of Judgment, the first question he is asked is not: 'Did you believe in God?' or 'Did you pray and perform ritual acts?'. But: 'Did you deal honourably and faithfully in your dealings with your fellow man?'

Talmud

IN THE hour when an individual is brought before the heavenly court for judgment, he is asked:
Did you conduct your affairs honestly?
Did you set aside regular time for Torah study?
Did you have children?
Did you look forward to the redemption of the world?

Talmud

ABBA OSHAY'YA, a laundryman, found some precious jewels in the linen which a queen had given him to wash. He gave them back. She said, 'They are yours. I have many others of more value.' He said: 'Our Law orders us to return what we have found.' She said: 'Blessed be the God of the Jews.'

Talmud

SHALL NOT the judge of all the earth do right?

Genesis 18:25

HE WHO deceives or lies to a person is as if he deceives or lies to God.

Sifre Numbers

RABBI GAMALIEL used to say: 'Act in secret as you act in public.'

Avot de-Rabbi Nathan

BEN BAG Bag said: 'You must not steal your own property back from a thief, lest you appear to be stealing.

Sifra

RABBI JANNAI said, 'It is not in our power to explain either the prosperity of the wicked or the tribulations of the righteous.'

Sayings of the Fathers

IF A man knows evidence favourable to another person, but witholds it, he is not legally liable to compensate that person. But Heaven will not pardon him until he does so.

Talmud

AFTER A trial ends, one of the judges, on leaving the court, should not say: 'I acquitted him: my colleagues convicted him. But what can I do? They outvoted me.' Of such a person it is written: 'Thou shalt not go about as a talebearer among my people.'

Talmud

IN A LAWSUIT you stand before God. When men came with a case before Rabbi Akiba, he said: 'Know before whom you stand. Not before me, Akiba, but before the Creator of the World.'

Talmud

THOU SHALT not wrest judgment; thou shalt not respect persons, neither take a gift: for a gift doth blind the eyes of the wise, and pervert the words of the righteous.

Deuteronomy 16:19

'GOD IS not a man that he should lie, or a mortal that he should repent' (*Numbers 23:19*). Samuel son of Nahmani said: 'When God promises good, he does not change his promise, come what may – unlike a mortal king who may withold a promised gift to his son if the son provokes him. God keeps his promise in spite of man's sin.'

Tanhuma

LIFE

LOVE

If love depends on some material cause, and the material cause passes away, the love vanishes. But if it does not depend on some material cause, it will never pass away.

Sayings of the Fathers

The root of love is to love the Lord. The soul is full of love, bound with the bounds of love in great joy. The joy chases away from his heart all bodily pleasures and worldly delights.

Eleazar ben Judah

Many waters cannot quench love, neither can the floods drown it.

Song of Songs 8:7

THOU SHALT love thy neighbour as thyself.

Leviticus 19:18

LET A man love God with a perfect love, whether it will go well or ill with him.

Tanna de be Eliyyahu

ONE WHO is incapable of love must learn how to flatter.

Yiddish Proverb

LIVING

TO EVERY thing there is a season, and a time to every purpose under the heaven:

A time to be born, and a time to die; a time to plant, and a time to pluck up that which is planted;

A time to kill, and a time to heal; a time to break down, and a time to build up;

A time to weep, and a time to laugh; a time to mourn, and a time to dance;

A time to cast away stones, and a time to gather stones together; a time to embrace, and a time to refrain from embracing;

A time to get, and a time to lose; a time to keep, and a time to cast away;

A time to rend, and a time to sew; a time to keep silence, and a time to speak;

A time to love, and a time to hate; a time of war, and a time of peace.

Ecclesiastes 3:1–8

THERE IS no new thing under the sun.

Ecclesiastes 1:9

SEE, I have set before thee this day life and good, and death and evil.

Deuteronomy 30:15

LIFE IS a passing shadow, says Scripture. Is it the shadow of a tower, of a tree? A shadow that lasts for a while? No, it is the shadow of a bird in its flight – away flies the bird, and there is neither bird nor shadow.

Talmud

VANITY OF vanities, saith the Preacher, vanity of vanities: all is vanity. What profit hath a man of all his labour which he taketh under the sun. One generation passeth away, and another generation cometh: but the earth abideth for ever.

Ecclesiastes 1:2–4

A MAN should so live that at the close of every day he can repeat: 'I have not wasted my day.'

Zohar

AKABIA BEN Mahalalel said, 'Reflect on three things and you will not transgress: know where you come from, where you are going, before whom you will in the future render an account and reckoning. "Where you come from" – from a fetid drop. "Where you are going" – to a place of dust, worms and maggots. "Before whom you will in future render an account and reckoning" – before the Supreme king of kings, the Holy One, blessed be he.'

Sayings of the Fathers

PEACE

HILLEL AND Shammai received (the tradition) from them. Hillel said, 'Be disciples of Aaron, loving peace and pursuing peace, loving fellow-creatures, and drawing them to the Law.'

Sayings of the Fathers

A PERSON should always be keen-witted in the fear of God, giving the soft answer that turns away wrath (*Proverbs 15:1*), increasing peace with his brothers and relatives and with all men, even the heathen in the street so that he may be beloved above, popular on earth, and acceptable to his fellow-creatures.

Talmud

BEHOLD, HOW good and how pleasant it is for brethren to dwell together in unity.

Psalm 133:1

RABBI SIMEON ben Gamaliel said: 'He who makes peace in his house, Scripture reckons it as if he made peace for every single Israelite in Israel. He who brings jealousy and strife into his house, is as if he brought them among all Israel.'

Avot de-Rabbi Nathan

AND HE shall judge among the nations, and shall rebuke many people: and they shall beat their swords into plowshares, and their spears into pruninghooks: nation shall not lift up sword against nation, neither shall they learn war any more.

Isaiah 2:4

AN INSINCERE peace is better than a sincere war.

Yiddish Proverb

THE WORST exile is exile from peace of mind.

Hasidic Tale

JOY

THE HOLY spirit does not rest where there is idleness, or sadness, or ribaldry, or frivolity, or empty speech. But only where there is joy.

Midrash Psalms

THANKSGIVING

DO NOT be like those who honour their gods in prosperity and curse them in adversity. Rather, in pleasure or pain, give thanks.

Mekhilta

HOPE

PREFER ONE in hand to two in hope.

BENEDICT OF OXFORD

HUMAN NATURE

HUMANITY

A PERSON'S nature can be recognized through three things: his cup, his purse, and his anger.

Talmud

YET MAN is born unto trouble, as the sparks fly upward.

Job 5:7

WHAT IS in your heart about your fellow man is most likely in his heart about you.

Sifre Deuteronomy

LORD, WHAT is man, that thou takest knowledge of him! or the son of man, that thou makest account of him! Man is like to vanity: his days are as a shadow that passeth away.

Psalm 144:3–4

RABBI HAGGAI said in the name of Rabbi Isaac: 'All need grace, even Abraham, for whose sake grace came plenteously into the world. He himself needed grace.'

Genesis Rabbah

WHOEVER SAVES one life, it is as if he saved the entire world.

Mishnah

RABBI ALEXANDER said: If a mortal man uses broken vessels, it is a disgrace. But with God it is otherwise, for all his servants are broken vessels.

Pesikta Kahana

A COMPANION can be gained only with the greatest difficulty. Thus they say: 'Let a man gain a companion for himself, one who will read with him, learn with him, eat and drink with him, and share his secrets. For two are better than one.'

Sifre Deuteronomy

RABBI JOSHUA ben Levi said: 'When a man goes on the road, a troop of angels proceeds in front of him and proclaims: "Make way for the image of the Holy One, blessed be he."'

Deuteronomy Rabbah

I GAVE my heart to seek and search out by wisdom concerning all things that are done under heaven: this sore travail hath God given to the sons of man to be exercised therewith. I have seen all the works that are done under the sun; and, behold, all is vanity and vexation of spirit.

Ecclesiastes 1:13–14

EVIL INCLINATION

THE WORDS of the Law are likened to a medicine of life. Like a king, who seriously woounded his son, and he then put a plaster on his wound. He said: 'My son, so long as this plaster is on your wound, eat and drink what you like, and wash in cold or warm water, and you will suffer no harm. But if you remove it, you will get a bad boil.' So God says to the Israelites: 'I created within you the evil inclination. But I created the Law as a medicine. As long as you occupy yourselves with the Law, the evil inclination will not rule over you. But if you do not occupy yourselves with the Torah, then you will be delivered into the power of the evil inclination, and all its power will be against you.'

Sifre Deuteronomy

RABA SAID: 'Even though God created the evil inclination, he created the Law as an antidote against it.'

Talmud

RABBI ILAI said: 'If a man finds that his evil inclination overmasters him, let him go to a place where nobody knows him, dress and cover himself in black, and act as his passion desires. But let him not profane the name of God in public.'

Talmud

THIS IS the device of the evil inclination: Today it says: 'Do this.' Tomorrow: 'Do that.' Until at last it says: 'Worship an idol', and a person goes and does it.

Talmud

SIN

TO A person who says: 'I will sin and repent', the Day of Atonement brings no forgiveness. For sins against God, the Day of Atonement brings forgiveness. But for sins against one's neighbour, the Day of Atonement brings no forgiveness until he has become reconciled with his neighbour.

Talmud

RAB SAID: 'Whoever commits a transgression and is filled with shame, all his sins are forgiven.

Talmud

RABBI HOSHAIAH said: 'He who possesses knowledge, but has not the fear of sin, possesses nothing. A craftsman who has no tools is no craftsman. The key which unlocks the Law is the fear of sin.'

Exodus Rabbah

COMMIT A sin twice, and you will think it perfectly allowable.

Talmud

TRANSGRESSION

A PERSON came to Raba and said: 'The leader of my town has ordered me to kill so and so, or he will kill me.' Raba replied: 'Let him kill you. Do not commit murder. Why should you think that your blood is redder than his? Perhaps his is redder than yours.'

Talmud

THE HOLY One hates him who says one thing in his mouth and another in his heart.

Talmud

IMMORALITY AT home is like a worm in the vegetables.

Talmud

DO NOT reproach another for a blemish that is in you.

RASHI

RABBI ELAZAR of Modim said, 'If one profane sacred things, and despise the Holydays, and put his fellow man to shame publicly, and make void the covenant of Abraham our father, peace be unto him, and cause the Law to have a meaning other than what is in accordance with traditional law, then even though knowledge of the Law and good deeds are his, he has no share in the world to come.'

Sayings of the Fathers

NOTHING IS more dangerous for a nation or for an individual than to plead guilty to imaginary sins.

AHAD HA'AM

BEN AZZAI said, 'Run to (fulfil even) a slight precept as (you would) a grave one, and flee from transgression. For one good deed brings about another, and one transgression leads to another transgression, since the recompense of a good deed is a good deed, whereas the reward of a transgression is a transgression.'

Sayings of the Fathers

IF A wicked man abandons his wickedness and repents, do not despise him.

Midrash Proverbs

SINNERS ARE mirrors. When we see faults in them, we should recognize that they only reflect the evil in us.

BAAL SHEM TOV

FOOLISHNESS

ONCE A Raman lady put this question to Rabbi Jose ben Halafta: 'Is it a fact that all God's praise consists in his "giving wisdom to the wise"? ' (*Daniel 2:21.*) 'It should rather be by giving wisdom to fools!' Jose said to her. 'Have you any jewels?' 'Certainly.' 'If someone comes and wishes to borrow them, will you lend them to him?' 'Yes, if he is a responsible person.' 'Then', said Rabbi Jose, 'you will only lend your jewels to a worthy borrower. Should God give his wisdom to fools?'

Tanhuma

THE FEAR of the Lord is the beginning of knowledge: but fools despise wisdom and instruction.

Proverbs 1:7

A REPROOF entereth more into a wise man than an hundred stripes into a fool.

Proverbs 17:10

WHO IS a pious man and yet a fool? He who sees a woman drowning and says: 'It is unseemly for me to look at her, therefore I cannot rescue her.'

Talmud

AVOID AS much as possible bad men, men of persistent angry feelings and fools. You can get nothing from their company but shame.

ASHER BEN YEHIEL

DEAD FLIES cause the ointment of the apothecary to send forth a stinking savour: so doth a little folly him that is in reputation for wisdom and honour.

Ecclesiastes 10:1

ONE COIN in a bottle rattles. A bottle full of coins makes no sound. So the scholar who is the son of a scholar is modest. But the scholar who is the son of an ignoramous trumpets his knowledge around.

Talmud

EVIL

IT IS because man is half angel, half brute, that his inner life witnesses such bitter war between such unlike natures.

MOSES OF COUCY

ENVY THOU not the oppressor, and choose none of his ways.

Proverbs 3:31

MANY SORROWS shall be to the wicked: but he that trusteth in the Lord, mercy shall compass him about.

Psalm 32:10

ENTER NOT into the path of the wicked, and go not in the way of evil men.

Proverbs 4:14

THERE IS no greater adultery than when a woman, while her husband has intercourse with her, thinks of another man.

Tanhuma

LUSTFUL THOUGHTS are even worse than lustful deeds.

Talmud

KEEP ME from sinful men and worthless companions.

Jewish Prayer Book

WICKEDNESS

THE PUNISHMENT for a liar is that even when he tells the truth, he is not believed.

Talmud

AS I like, saith the Lord God, I have no pleasure in the death of the wicked; but that the wicked turn from his way and live.

Ezekiel 33:11

RIGHTEOUSNESS

RIGHTEOUS ACTIONS

ALEXANDER THE Great came across a simple people in Africa who did not wage war. He lingered to learn their ways. Two citizens appeared before the chief with this point of contention: One had bought a piece of land and discovered a treasure in it; he claimed that this belonged to the seller, and wished to return it. The seller, on the other hand, declared that he sold the land with all it might contain. So he refused to accept the treasure. The chief, turning to the buyer said: 'Thou has a son?' 'Yes.' And addressing the seller, 'Thou hast a daughter?' 'Yes.' 'Marry one to the other and make the treasure their marriage settlement.' They left content. 'In my country,' said Alexander, 'the disputants would have been imprisoned, and the treasure confiscated for the king.' 'Is your country blessed by sun and rain?' asked the chief. 'Yes,' replied Alexander. 'Does it contain cattle?' 'Yes.' 'Then it must be for the sake of these innocent annimals that the sun shines upon it; surely its people are unworthy of such blessing.'

Talmud

LET JUSTICE flow down as waters, and righteousness as a mighty stream.

Amos 5:24

THOSE THAT be planted in the house of the Lord shall flourish in the courts of our God. They shall still bring forth fruit in old age; they shall be fat and flourishing. To shew that the Lord is upright: he is my rock, and there is no unrighteousness in him.

Psalm 93:13–14

BE THE cursed; not he who curses. Be of those who are persecuted, not of those who persecute.

Talmud

HE HATH showed thee, O man, what is good; and what doth the Lord require of thee, but to do justly, and to love mercy, and to walk humbly with thy God.

Micah 6:8

RABBI SIMAI says that with regard to all the creatures who were created from heaven, their bodies and souls are heavenly. Whereas all the creatures that were created from the earth, their bodies and souls are earthly. Man however is the exception. His body is earthly, but his soul is heavenly. Therefore if a man fulfils the Law and does the will of his father in heaven, he is like the creatures above. But if not, then he is like the creatures below.

Sifre Deuteronomy

THE DEATH of the righteous weighs as heavily as the burning of the Temple.

Talmud

A GOOD name is rather to be chosen than great riches, and loving favour rather than silver and gold.

Proverbs 22:1

THE RIGHTEOUS are masters of their passions. Not so the wicked: they are the slaves of their desires.

Talmud

HILLEL USED to say: Whatever is hateful unto thee, do it not unto thy fellow. This is the whole law; the rest is commentary.

Talmud

PIETY

A MAN should not be jokey or frivolous. Nor should he be sad or gloomy. He should be calm. Our wise men declare: Jokes and frivolity lead a man to lewdness. They say that a man should not laugh or grieve or mourn too easily, but should meet everyone with a cheerful expression. Also a man should not be over-ambitious or too eager to do well. Nor should he be too pessimistic so that he never accomplishes anything ... He should not be quick to quarrel, or envy the good fortune of others, or be lecherous or anxious for fame.

MOSES MAIMONIDES

FIRST IMPROVE yourself. Then improve others.

Talmud

REPENTANCE

THESE ARE man's intercessors: repentance and good deeds.

Talmud

AS SOILED garments can be cleansed, so the Israelites – even though they sin – can return through repentance to the Lord.

Exodus Rabbah

A KING had a son who had gone astray from his father on a journey of a hundred days. His friends said to him: 'Return to your father.' He said: 'I cannot.' Then his father sent him a message. 'Return as far as you can, and I will come to you the rest of the way.' So God says: 'Return to me, and I will return to you.'

Pesikta Rabbati

THE END of wisdom is repentance and good deeds.

Talmud

GOD SAYS, 'My hands are stretched out towards the penitent. I reject no creature who gives me his heart in penitence.' Therefore it says: 'Peace, peace to the far and to the near. To all who draw near to me, I draw near and heal them.'

Midrash Psalms

BE NOT like the fools who, when they sin, bring an offering but do not repent. They do not know the difference between good and evil. Yet they venture to make an offering to God.

Talmud

SO HOW wonderful a thing is repentance! God says, 'If you return to me, I will return to you.' (*Malachi 3:7*). For however many sins a man may have committed, if he return to God, they are all forgiven. He accounts it to him as though he had not sinned (*Ezekiel 18:22*). But if he does not return, God warns him once, twice, three times. Then, if the man does not return, God exacts punishment.

Tanhuma

PURITY

IF A man is pure and upright in deed, and if he grasps the cords of love existing in the holy roots of his soul, he will be able to ascend to every level in the whole supernal universe.

MOSES CORDOVERO

DUTY

RABBI USED to say: If you have done God's will as your will, you have not done his will as his will.

Avot de-Rabbi Nathan

FEAR OF GOD

THE ROOT of the fear of the Lord is when a man desires something and yet he gives up the pleasure for which his evil inclination craves because he fears the Lord.

ELEAZAR BEN JUDAH

AT ALL times let a man fear God in private as in public, acknowledge the truth, and speak the truth in his heart.

Jewish Prayer Book

HONOUR

RABBI ELAZAR ben Shammua said, 'Let the honour of your disciple be as precious to you as your own.'

Sayings of the Fathers

HE WHO welcomes an old man is as if he welcomed the Divine Presence.

Genesis Rabbah

RABBI SIMON said, 'There are three crowns: the crown of (the study of) the Law, the crown of priesthood, and the crown of royalty. Yet the crown of a good name surpasses them all.'

Sayings of the Fathers

RABBI ELIEZER said: 'Let the honour of your neighbour be as dear to you as your own. As a man has pleasure in his own honour, let him have pleasure in the honour of his neighbour.'

Avot de-Rabbi Nathan

THOU SHALT rise up before the hoary head, and honour the face of the old man, and fear thy God: I am the Lord.

Leviticus 19:32

TRUST IN GOD

THE LORD is my light and my salvation. Whom shall I fear?

Psalm 27:1

BLESSED IS the man that trusteth in the Lord, and whose hope the Lord is. For he shall be as a tree planted by the waters, and that spreadeth out her roots by the river, and shall not see when heat cometh, but her leaf shall be green; and shall not be careful in the year of drought, neither shall cease from yielding fruit.

Jeremiah 17:7–8

THE LORD is nigh unto all who call upon him, to all that call upon him in truth.

Psalm 145:18

DOUBT

I SHOULD like to explain why people have doubts, deny miracles and lose their faith in God ... Firstly, people are usually reluctant to think deeply about matters. Therefore when they meet something that might strengthen their faith in the Torah, they are frightened and run away from it. Because of this you find people saying that truth is hard, or that truth is bitter. They do not want to be involved in the whole business and so they run away. Secondly is the fact that many people are stupid and talk foolishly and seem bent on idleness. So whenever they meet a valuable idea, they satisfy their inner conscience by insisting that there is nothing in it. The third cause of religious doubt is that man is determined to satisfy his desire for food, drink, possessions and sexual satisfaction. He is so preoccupied with these things that he gives no thought to anything else ... The fourth cause ... is that people are indifferent and unreflective when they come across a true idea ... The fifth cause ... is human pride and contempt. Once these vices take possession of a man, they stop him from admitting his ignorance on any matter of philosophy ... the sixth cause ... is the result of hearing the words of an unbeliever ... The seventh cause of religious doubt is the result of hearing a feeble argument in support of faith. He sees that the argument is nonsense and therefore he thinks all the arguments of believers should be ridiculed. The eighth cause of religious doubt is the result of personal hatred of individual believers. This hatred can lead to a hatred of the God in whom they believe.

SAADIAH GAON

HUMILITY

SHAME-STRICKEN, bending low,
My God, I come before thee, for I know
That even as thou on high
Exalted are in power and majesty,
So weak and frail am I:
That perfect as thou art,
So I deficient am in every part.

SOLOMON IBN GABIROL

BE NOT righteous over much; neither make thyself over wise: why shouldest thou destroy thyself? Be not over much wicked, neither be thou foolish: why shouldest thou die before thy time?

Ecclesiastes 7:16–17

WISDOM BEGETS humility.

ABRAHAM IBN EZRA

HE WHO humiliates himself will be lifted up, but he who raises himself up will be humiliated.

Talmud

DO NOT resemble a big door, which lets in the wind, or a small door, which makes the worthy bend down. But instead resemble the threshold on which all may tread, or a low peg on which all can hang their things.

Derek Erez Zuta

GOD LOVES nothing better than modesty.

Pesikta Rabbati

BE NOT rash with thy mouth, and let not thine heart be hasty to utter any thing before God: for God is in heaven, and thou upon earth: therefore let thy words be few.

Ecclesiastes 5:2

IF A pupil is ill, and the teacher goes to visit him, the other pupils go before to announce the teacher's coming. But when God went to visit Abraham when he was ill, he went first before the angels. (*Genesis 18:1–2.*) Is there anyone more humble than he?

Tanhuma

O GOD, I stand before thee, knowing all my deficiencies, and overwhelmed by thy greatness and majesty.

BAHYA IBN PAKUDAH

TEACH YOUR tongue to say: 'I do not know' lest you be led to lie.

Talmud

DEEDS

CHARITY

GIVING IS not the essential thing, but to give with delicacy of feeling.

Talmud

WHOSOEVER WITHOLDS alms from the needy thereby withdraws himself from the lustre of the Shekhinah (Divine Presence) and the light of the Law.

JACOB BEN ASHER

EVEN A poor man who survives on charity should give charity.

Talmud

TO HIM for whom bread is suitable, give bread. To him who needs dough, give dough. To him for whom money is required, give money. To him for whom it is fitting to put the food in his mouth, put it in.

Sifre Deuteronomy

THERE ARE four kinds of people who give to charity. One is willing to contribute himself, but he does not want others to give. He is jealous of what belongs to others. Another is willing that others give, but is unwilling to contribute himself. He is jealous of what belongs to himself. Then there is the one who both gives himself and wants others to give – he is a righteous man, and there is the man who neither gives himself, nor wants others to give. He is wicked.

Sayings of the Fathers

ONE WHO gives charity in secret is greater than Moses.

Talmud

THERE ARE eight levels in the giving of charity, each one higher than the other. The highest level ... is to help a Jew who has been crushed by giving him a gift or by taking him into partnership or by finding such work for him that he is put back on his feet and no longer depends on charity ... The second level is the man who gives charity to the poor. He does not know to whom he is giving while the recipient does not know from whom he is receiving ... the third level is when the donor knows the recipient, but the poor man does not know the donor ... the fourth level is when the poor man knows from whom he is receiving, but the donor does not know to whom he is giving ... the fifth level is when a man gives even before he is asked ... the sixth level is when a man gives after he has been asked ... the seventh level is when a man gives less than he should, but gives graciously, and at the lowest level is the man who gives reluctantly.

MOSES MAIMONIDES

IF A person closes his eyes to avoid giving charity, it is as though he committed adultery.

Talmud

COMPASSION

THOU SHALT neither vex a stranger, nor oppress him: for ye were strangers in the land of Egypt.

Exodus 22:21

RABBI JUDAH the Prince was sitting studying the Torah in front of the synagogue in Sepphoris when a calf passed before him on its way to slaughter. It began to cry out as though saying: 'Save me!' He replied: 'What can I do for you? It is for this that you were fashioned.' As a punishment he suffered toothache for thirteen years. One day a creeping thing ran past his daughter who tried to kill it. He said: 'My daughter, let it alone, for it is written: "His mercies are over all his works."' (*Psalm 145:9*.) Immediately he was restored to health.

Genesis Rabbah

GOD GLORIFIES the offering of the poor.

Pesikta Rabbati

VISIT THE sick and suffering man, and let your countenance be cheerful when he sees it.

ELIEZER BEN ISAAC

A MAN must not give presents to someone when he knows they will not be accepted.

JUDAH HEHASID

GOD IS on the watch for the nations of the world to repent, so that he can bring them under his wings.

Numbers Rabbah

RABBI JOSHUA ben Nehemiah said: 'Have you ever seen it happen that the rain fell on the field of a person who was righteous, and not on the field of a person who was wicked? Or that the sun arose and shone upon Israel who was righteous, and not upon the wicked? God causes the sun to shine both upon Israel and upon the nations, because the Lord is good to all.

Pesikta Rabbati

RABBI TANHUMA ben Abba cited Proverbs 11:30: 'He that is wise, wins souls.' The rabbis said: 'This refers to Noah, for in the ark he fed and sustained the animals with much care. He gave to each animal its special food, and fed each at its proper period – some in the daytime and some at night. Thus he gave chopped straw to the camel, barley to the ass, vine tendrils to the elephant, and glass to the ostrich. So for twelve months he did not sleep by night or day, because all the time he was busy feeding the animals.'

Tanhuma

WHEN MOSES was feeding the sheep of his father-in-law in the wilderness, a young kid ran away. Moses pursued it until it reached a ravine where it found a well to drink from. When Moses reached it, he said, 'I did not know that you ran away because you were thirsty. Now you must be weary.' He carried the kid back. Then God said, 'Because you have shown pity in leading back one of a flock belonging to a man, you shall lead my flock, Israel.'

Exodus Rabbah

RABBI JUDAH said in the name of Rab: 'A man is forbidden to eat anything until he has fed his beast.'

Talmud

ALL MEN are responsible for each other.

Talmud

IT WAS revealed to the rabbis in a dream that a certain man in a certain village should pray that rain might come. So they sent for him. They asked him what was his trade. He replied that he was an ass-driver. Then they said: 'Have you ever done any good deed in your life?' He replied: 'Once I hired an ass to a woman who began to weep on the road. I asked her why she wept. She told me that her husband was in prison and that she was going to the city to sell her chastity to obtain his ransom. When he came to the city, I sold my ass, gave her the money I received, and said to her: "Take this, free your husband, and do not sin."' The rabbis said to him: 'Worthy indeed are you to pray for us and be answered.' The man prayed, and rain fell.

Talmud

BEFORE HE brought the flood, God himself kept seven days of mourning. For he was grieved at heart.

Tanhuma

IT IS taught in the name of Rabbi Joshua: The poor man does more for the rich man than the rich man does for the poor.

Ruth Rabbah

WHEN THE daughters of Zelophehad (*Numbers 27:1–12*) heard that the land was being divided among men to the exclusion of women, they assembled together to take counsel. They said: 'The compassion of God is not as the compassion of men. The compassion of men extends to men more than to women, but not thus is the compassion of God. His compassion extends equally to men and women and to all, even as it is said: "The Lord is good to all, and his mercies are over all his works." ' (*Psalm 145:9*)

Sifre Numbers

MERCY

NOW A man is more merciful to men than to women – but God's mercies are over all his creatures (*Psalm 145:9*). So Moses added the words 'all the people of Israel', and continued, 'your little ones, your wives, and the stranger that is in your camp,' since God's mercies are on male and female alike, on the wicked equally with the righteous. As it says, 'From the hewer of your wood to the drawer of your water.' All are equal before God. Hence it says, 'All the people of Israel'.

Tanhuma

AS GOD is called merciful and gracious, be merciful and gracious – offering gifts freely to all. As the Lord is called righteous and loving, be righteous and loving.

Sifre Deuteronomy

IF GOD is merciful to those who sin against his will, how much more merciful will he be to those who do his will.

Sifre Numbers

A PERSON to whom a terrible event has occurred should make it known publicly so that many people may entreat God's mercy on his behalf.

Talmud

RABBI GALMALIEL said: 'So long as you are merciful, God will have mercy upon you. But if you are not merciful, he will not be merciful to you.'

Talmud

DEBT

DO NOT tell the collector: 'It was a mistake.' This refers to someone who makes a public pledge of charity and then refuses to pay. Do not tell the charity collector when he comes: 'I did not really mean what I said. My pledge was not meant to be taken in earnest. I only spoke out so as to avoid public embarrassment, or so others may pledge. But I did not and I do not intend to give any of my own money.' Or perhaps you will say: 'I did not know what I was doing.' Or, 'At the time I made the pledge I was confident I would be able to pay, but now I find I cannot.' None of these excuses will be acceptable to God.

Midrash Psalms

IT IS forbidden to cross a road to meet a man who is your debtor, and who you know cannot pay you. It is as if he were tortured with fire and water.

Talmud

OUR GOD, our father, be our shepherd and feed us. Provide for us, sustain and support us. Relieve us speedily from all our troubles. Let us never be in need of charity of our fellow men nor their loans. Rather let us be dependent on your hand alone which is full, open, holy and ample. So shall we never lose our self-respect nor be put to shame.

Grace after Meals

חג המצות
באורך נראה אור
להדליק נר של יום טוב
פסח
והגדת לבנך ביום ההוא

UNSELFISHNESS

ANTIGONUS OF Socho received (the tradition) from Simon the Just. He used to say, 'Do not be like servants that minister to the master on the condition of receiving a reward. Instead be like servants that minister to the master without the condition of receiving a reward. And let the fear of heaven be upon you.'

Sayings of the Fathers

HILLEL USED to say, 'If I am not for myself, who will be for me? But if I am only for myself, what am I? And if not now, when?'

Sayings of the Fathers

WORK

WHATSOEVER THY hand findeth to do, do it with thy might.

Ecclesiastes 9:10

GO TO the ant, thou sluggard; consider her ways, and be wise.

Proverbs 6:6

GREAT IS labour – it confers honour on the labourer.

Talmud

RABBI TARFON said, 'The day is short, the task is great, the labourers are sluggish, the recompense is ample, and the Master of the house is urgent.'

Sayings of the Fathers

MODERATION

RICHES

DO NOT make gold the foremost longing of your life for that is the first step to idolatry.

ASHER BEN YEHIEL

GOLD AND silver take a man out of this world and the world to come. But the Torah brings a man to the life of the world to come.

Sifre Numbers

A GOOD name is rather to be chosen than great riches, and loving favour rather than silver and gold.

Proverbs 22:1

WEALTH GOTTEN by vanity shall be diminished; but he that gathereth by labour shall increase.

Proverbs 13:11

POSSESSIONS

I MADE me great works: I builded me houses; I planted me vineyards: I made me gardens and orchards and I planted trees in them of all kind of fruits: I made me pools of water, to water therewith the wood that bringeth forth trees: I got me servants and maidens, and had servants born in my house; also I had great possessions of great and small cattle above all that were in Jerusalem before me: I gathered me also silver and gold, and the peculiar treasure of kings and of the provinces: I got me men singers and women singers, and the delights of the sons of men, as musical instruments, and that of all sorts. So I was great, and increased more than all that were before me in Jerusalem: also my wisdom remained with me. And whatsoever mine eyes desired I kept not from them, I withheld not my heart from any joy; for my heart rejoiced in all my labour: and this was my portion of all my labour. Then I looked on all the works that my hands had wrought, and on the labour that I had laboured to do: and, behold, all was vanity and vexation of spirit, and there was no profit under the sun.

Ecclesiastes 2:4–11

LAY THIS well to heart, reflect on it again and again; that which is superfluous is without end.

MOSES MAIMONIDES

GREED

WHOEVER LOVETH silver shall not be satisfied with silver; nor he that loveth abundance with increase.

Ecclesiastes 5:10

BE NOT thou envious against evil men, neither desire to be with them.

Proverbs 24:1

HE THAT oppresseth the poor to increase his riches, and he that giveth to the rich, shall surely come to want.

Proverbs 22:16

ASCETICISM

RABBI JEREMIAH ben Abba said in the name of Resh Lakish: 'A scholar is not allowed to impose fasts upon himself, because it makes him lessen his heavenly work.'

Talmud

MODERATE ACTS

THE DIVINE religion does not urge us to lead an ascetic life, but guides us in the middle path, equidistant from the extremes of too much and too little.

YEHUDAH HALEVI

IT IS forbidden to accustom oneself to flattery. A man must beware of saying what he does not mean, and instead must say whatever is in his heart – his speech should reflect his beliefs.

JUDAH HEHASID

BE NOT hasty in thy spirit to be angry

Ecclesiastes 7:9

A SOFT answer turneth away wrath: but grievous words stir up anger.

Proverbs 15:1

IT IS better to hear the rebuke of the wise, than for a man to hear the song of fools.

Ecclesiastes 7:5

THY FRIEND has a friend, and thy friend's friend has a friend: be discreet.

Talmud

BE NOT rash with thy mouth, and let not thine heart be hasty to utter anything before God.

Ecclesiastes 5:2

LET ANOTHER man praise thee, and not thine own mouth; a stranger, and not thine own lips.

Proverbs 27:2

EAT THOU not the bread of him that hath an evil eye, neither desire thou his dainty meats.

Proverbs 23:6

DRINK

HE, WHO, in order to guard against sin, abstains from wine, is worthy to receive all the blessings contained in the Priestly benediction.

Numbers Rabbah

WINE IS a mocker, strong drink is raging: and whosoever is deceived thereby is not wise.

Proverbs 20:1

PLEASURE

FOR THEY said within themselves, reasoning not aright,
'Short and sorrowful is our life;
And there is no healing when a man cometh to his end,
And none was ever known that returned out of Hades.
Because by mere chance were we born,
And hereafter we shall be as though we had never been:
And our name shall be forgotten in time,
And no man shall remember our works;
And our life shall pass away as the traces of a cloud,
And shall be scattered as is a mist.
For our allotted time is the passing of a shadow,
And there is no putting back of our end.
Come therefore and let us enjoy the good things that now are;
And let us use the creation with all our soul as youth's possession.

Let us fill ourselves with costly wine and perfumes;
And let no flower of spring pass us by:
Let us crown ourselves with rosebuds, before they be withered:
Let none of us go without his share in our proud revelry:
Everywhere let us leave tokens of our mirth:
Because this is our portion, and our lot is this.
Let our strength be to us a law of righteousness;
For that which is weak is convicted to be of no service.'
Thus reasoned they, and they were led astray;
For their wickedness blinded them,
And they knew not the mysteries of God,
Neither hoped they for wages of holiness,
Nor did they judge that there is a prize for blameless souls.
Because God created man for incorruption,
And made him an image of his own everlastingness.

Wisdom of Solomon 2: 1–2, 4–9, 11, 21–3

RABBI JUDAH the Prince said: 'He who accepts the pleasures of this world is deprived of the pleasures of the world to come, and vice versa.'

Avot de-Rabbi Nathan

I SAID in my heart, Go to now, I will prove thee with mirth, therefore enjoy pleasure: and, behold, this also is vanity.

Ecclesiastes 2:1

FAMILY

WIVES AND HUSBANDS

AND THE Lord God said, It is not good that the man should be alone.

Genesis 2:18

RABBI SENT envoys to propose marriage to the widow (of Rabbi Eleazar, son of Rabbi Simeon). She sent back the message: Shall a basin which has held holy food be used for profane purposes?

Talmud

THEREFORE SHALL a man leave his father and his mother, and shall cleave unto his wife: and they shall be one flesh.

Genesis 2:24

A MAN must always be very careful to show honour to his wife.

Talmud

A MAN should love his wife as himself and honour her more than himself.

Talmud

BE CAREFUL not to cause a woman to weep, for God counts her tears.

Talmud

WHO CAN find a virtuous woman? For her price is far above rubies. The heart of her husband doth safely trust in her, so that he shall have no need of spoil. She will do him good and not evil all the days of her life … Strength and honour are her clothing; and she shall rejoice in time to come. She openeth her mouth with wisdom; and in her tongue is the law of kindness. She looketh well to the ways of her household, and eateth not the bread of idleness. Her children arise up, and call her blessed; her husband also, and he praiseth her. Many daughters have done virtuously, but thou excellest them all.

Proverbs 31:10–12, 25–29

RABBI JACOB said: He who has no wife lives without good, or help, or joy, or blessing, or atonement.

Genesis Rabbah

THERE WAS once a pious man who was married to a pious woman, and they had no children. They said, 'We are no profit to God.' So they divorced one another. The man went and married a bad woman, and she made him bad. But the woman went and married a bad man, and she made him good. Thus all depends on the woman.

Genesis Rabbah

RABBI JOHANAN said: If a man's first wife dies, it is as if the Temple were destroyed in his day.

Talmud

WHOEVER MARRIES a woman for her money will have disreputable children.

Talmud

RABBI HELBO said: 'Be careful about the honour of your wife, for blessing enters the house only because of the wife.

Talmud

RABBI ALEXANDRI said: If a man's wife dies, the world becomes dark for him.

Talmud

MOTHERS AND FATHERS

JEWISH CUSTOM bids the Jewish mother, after her preparations for the Sabbath have been completed on Friday evening, to kindle the Sabbath lamp. That is symbolic of the Jewish woman's influence on her own home, and through it upon larger circles. She is the inspirer of a pure, chaste, family life whose hallowing influences are incalculable; she is the centre of all spiritual endeavours, the confidante and fosterer of every undertaking. To her the Talmudic sentence applies: 'It is woman alone through whom God's blessings are vouchsafed to a house.'

HENRIETTA SZOLD

WHEN A child in his play breaks something valuable, his mother does not love the breakage. But if later on her son goes far away or dies she thinks of the incident with infinite tenderness because she now sees it only as one of the signs of her child's existence.

SIMONE WEIL

A MAN should never impose an overpowering fear on his household.

Talmud

THE FATHERS shall not be put to death for the children, neither shall the children be put to death for the fathers: every man shall be put to death for his own sin.

Deuteronomy 24:16

ONE DAY Rabbi Tarfon's mother's sandals split and broke, and as she could not mend them, she had to walk across the courtyard barefoot. So Rabbi Tarfon kept stretching his hands under her feet, so that she might walk over them all the way.

Talmud

HEAR, YE children, the instruction of a father, and attend to know understanding. For I give you good doctrine, forsake ye not my law.

Proverbs 4:1–2

THE RABBIS say: Three combine in the making of human beings: God, father and mother. If men honour their father and mother, God says: 'I reckon it to them as if I dwelt among them, and as if they honoured me.'

Talmud

HONOUR THY father and thy mother: that thy days may be long upon the land which the Lord thy God giveth thee.

Exodus 20:12

IT IS written: 'You shall reverence father and mother, Thou shalt reverence the Lord thy God.' Thus Scripture puts the reverence of parents side by side with the reverence of God.

Talmud

CHILDREN

YOUR SON at five is your master. At ten your servant. At fifteen your double. After that, your friend or foe depending on his bringing up.

HASDAI CRESCAS

THE BEST security for old age: respect your children.

SHOLEM ASCH

A FATHER complained to the Baal Shem Tov that his son had turned away from God and asked what he should do. The Baal Shem Tov replied: Love him more than ever.

AARON OF APT

RABBI JUDAH says: 'Whoever does not teach his son a trade or profession teaches him to be a thief.'

Talmud

HE THAT gathereth in summer is a wise son; but he that sleepeth in harvest is a son that causeth shame.

Proverbs 10:5

THEY THAT are planted in the house of the Lord (*Psalm 92:13*). Rabbi Hanan ben Pazzi said: 'While they are saplings, they are in the house of the Lord – these are the little children who are in school.'

Numbers Rabbah

'TOUCH NOT mine anointed, and do my prophets no harm.' (*I Chronicles 16:22.*) The former are schoolchildren. The latter, rabbis. Rabbi Lakish said in the name of Rabbi Judah Nesiah: 'The world stands only upon the breath of the schoolchildren.' Rabbi Papa said to Abbai: 'How about your breath and mine?' Abbai replied: 'the breath of them that are sinful cannot be compared with the breath of them that are not sinful.' Resh Lakish said in the name of Rabbi Judah Nesiah: 'Let not the children be kept back from school, even to help in building of the Temple.'

Talmud

'HE HAS set the world in their heart.' (*Ecclesiastes 3:11*). Rabbi Jonathan interpreted the words to refer to the love of children which God has put in men's hearts. Like a king who had two sons – the elder honoured him; the younger was corrupt, and yet he loved the younger more than the elder.

Ecclesiastes Rabbah

TRAIN UP a child in the way he should go: and when he is old, he will not depart from it.

Proverbs 22:6

ONE SHOULD not promise to give something to a child and then not give it to him. As a result the child will learn to lie.

Talmud

MY SON, forget not my law; but let thine heart keep my commandments. For length of days, and long life, and peace, shall they add to thee.

Proverbs 3:1–2

THE LOVE of parents goes to their children, but the love of these children goes to their children.

Talmud

MY SON, if thou wilt receive my words, and hide my commandments with thee; So that thou incline thine ear unto wisdom, and apply thine heart to understanding; Yea, if thou criest after knowledge, and liftest up thy voice for understanding; If thou seekest her as silver, and searchest for her as for hid treasures; Then shalt thou understand the fear of the Lord, and find the knowledge of God.

Proverbs 2:1–4

'EAT THY bread with joy.' (*Ecclesiastes 9:7.*) Rabbi Huna ben Aha said: 'When children leave school, a heavenly voice calls out: "Eat thy bread with joy. The breath of your lips is received before me as a sweet savour." And when the Israelites leave their synagogues and houses of study, a heavenly voice declares: "Eat your bread with joy. Your prayers have been heard before me as a sweet savour." '

Ecclesiastes Rabbah

RABBI HAMNUNA said: 'Jerusalem was destroyed only because children did not attend school and instead loitered in the streets.'

Talmud

RABBI JUDAH said: 'See how beloved are the little children before God. When the Sanhedrin went into captivity, the *shekhinah* (Divine Presence) went not with them. When the watchers of the priests went into captivity, the Divine Presence did not go with them. But when the little children went into captivity, the Divine Presence went with them. For it says in *Lamentations 1:5*: "Her children are gone into captivity", and immediately after it in *Lamentations 1:6*: "From Zion her splendour is departed." '

Lamentations Rabbah

RABBI ISSACHAR said of a child who says Masha for Moses, Ahran for Aaron, and Aphron for Ephron, that God says: 'Even his stammering I love.'

Song of Songs Rabbah

HOME

THE JEW'S home has rarely been his 'castle'. Throughout the ages it has been something far higher – his sanctuary.

J.H. HERTZ

COURAGE

SALVATION

THE LORD is my shepherd; I shall not want.
He maketh me to lie down in green pastures; he leadeth me beside the still waters.
He restoreth my soul: he leadeth me in the paths of righteousness for his name's sake.
Yea, though I walk through the valley of the shadow of death. I will fear no evil: for thou art with me; thy rod and thy staff they comfort me.
Thou preparest a table before me in the presence of mine enemies: thou anointest my head with oil; my cup runneth over.
Surely goodness and mercy shall follow me all the days of my life: and I will dwell in the house of the Lord for ever.

Psalm 23:1–6

THE LORD is my light and my salvation; whom shall I fear?

Psalm 27:1

GOD IS our refuge and strength, a very present help in trouble. Therefore will not we fear, though the earth be removed, and though the mountains be carried into the midst of the sea. Though the waters thereof roar and be troubled, though the mountains shake with the swelling thereof.

Psalm 46:1–3

AS FOR God, his way is perfect; the word of the Lord is tried: he is a buckler to all of them that trust in him.

II Samuel 22:31

WHEN MY father and my mother forsake me, then the Lord will take me up.

Psalm 27:10

THE SPIRIT of a man will sustain his infirmity; but a wounded spirit who can bear?

Proverbs 18:14

BRAVERY

BE A man in your youth. But if you are then defeated in the struggle, return, return at last to God however old you are.

ELEAZAR OF WORMS

ADVERSITY

WHEN TROUBLE comes upon the congregation, it is not right for a man to say, 'I will eat and drink, and things will be peaceful for me.' Moses, our teacher, always bore his share in the troubles of the congregation.

Talmud

SALVATION IS attained not by subscription to metaphysical dogmas, but solely by love of God that fulfils itself in action.

HASDAI CRESCAS

SUFFERING

YEA, THEY slay us and they smite,
Vex our souls with sore affright;
All the closer cleave we, Lord,
To think everlasting word.
Not a word of all their Mass
Shall our lips in homage pass;
Though they curse, and bind, and kill,
The living God is with us still.
We still are thine, though limbs are torn;
Better death than life foresworn.
Noblest matrons seek for death,
Rob their children of their breath;
Fathers, in their fiery zeal,
Slay their sons with murderous steel,
And in heat of holiest strife,
For love of thee, spare not their life.
The fair and young lie down to die
In witness of thy unity;
From dying lips the accents swell,
'Thy God is One, O Israel';
And bridegroom answers unto bride,
'The Lord is God, and none beside'.

And, knit with bonds of holiest faith,
They pass to endless life through death.

KALONYMOS BEN YEHUDAH

RABBI JOSHUA ben Levi said: 'He who accepts gladly the sufferings of this world brings salvation to the world.'

Talmud

BEN HAI Hai said, 'According to the suffering is the reward.'

Sayings of the Fathers

THERE IS, if one many say so, no rejoicing before God at the destruction of the wicked. But if there is no rejoicing before him at the death of the wicked, how much less at the death of the righteous, of whom even one is worth the whole world.

Mekhilta

WHY IS it that there is a righteous person who enjoys good and there is a righteous person who suffers? It is because in the latter case the righteous person was formerly wicked and for this reason he is punished. But is one punished for offences committed during one's youth? ... I do not refer to the misdeeds in the course of a person's life. I refer to the fact that a person pre-existed prior to his present life.

Bahir

HE WAS despised and rejected of men; a man of sorrows, and acquainted with grief: and we hid as it were our faces from him; he was despised, and we esteemed him not.

Surely he hath borne our griefs, and carried our sorrows: yet we did esteem him stricken, smitten of God, and afflicted.

But he was wounded for our transgressions, he was bruised for our iniquities: the chastisement of our peace was upon him; and with his stripes we are healed.

He was oppressed, and he was afflicted, yet he opened not his mouth: he is brought as a lamb to the slaughter, and as a sheep before her shearers is dumb, so he openeth not his mouth.

Isaiah 53:3–5, 7

EVEN WHEN the gates of heaven are shut to prayer, they are open to tears.

Talmud

WISDOM

STUDY

ON A certain occasion Rabbi Eliezer used all the arguments in the world to prove his opinion concerning a point of law. But the rabbis refused to accept it. Finally, he said: 'If I am right about this law, let this carob tree prove it.' The carob tree uprooted itself and moved a hundred cubits. The rabbis said: 'No proof can be brought from a carob tree!'

Rabbi Eliezer said: 'If I am right about this law, let this stream prove it.' Then the stream turned about and flowed backwards. The rabbis said to him: 'No proof can be brought from a stream.'

Rabbi Eliezer said, 'If I am right about this law, let the walls of this House of Study prove it.' The walls of the House of Study began to bend inwards as if about to fall. Rabbi Joshua rebuked them, saying: 'If the students of the wise are disputing about the law, what does it have to do with you!' Out of respect for Rabbi Joshua the walls did not fall, but out of respect for Rabbi Eliezer they did not straighten up, but remained bent to this day.

Rabbi Eliezer said: 'If I am right about this law, may proof come from heaven.' A voice came out from heaven and said:

'What have you to do with Rabbi Eliezer? On every occasion he is right about the interpretation of the law.' Rabbi Joshua stood up and said: 'It is not in heaven' (*Deuteronomy 30:12*). What did he mean by using this quotation? Rabbi Jeremiah said: 'The Torah was already given to us on Mount Sinai. We pay no attention to a heavenly voice for you have already written in the Torah at Sinai: 'Decide according to the majority' (*Exodus 23:22*). Rabbi Nathaan met the prophet Elijah and asked him: 'What did the Holy One, blessed be he, do in that hour?' Elijah said: 'He was laughing and saying: "My children have defeated me! My children have defeated me!" '

Talmud

AT THE time of his dying, Rabbi raised ten fingers to Heaven and said: 'Lord of the Universe, you know and it has been revealed to you that I have laboured in the study of the Torah with my ten fingers, and that I did not enjoy any worldly advantage even with my little finger. May there be peace in my resting place, according to your will.' A voice from Heaven echoed saying, 'He shall enter into peace.'

Talmud

BEN BAG Bag said, 'Turn it (the Law) and turn it over again, for everything is therein.'

Sayings of the Fathers

UNTIL WHAT period in life ought one to study Torah? Until the day of one's death.

MOSES MAIMONIDES

AS A little wood can ignite a large tree, so young pupils sharpen the wits of great scholars. Hence Rabbi Hanina said: 'Much Torah have I learnt from my teachers, more from my colleagues, but from my students most of all.'

Talmud

RABBI ELISHA ben Abuyah said that a man who has learnt much Torah and has good deeds is like a horse which has reins. The man who has the first but not the second is like a horse without reins. It soon throws the rider over its head.

Avot de-Rabbi Nathan

RABBI SIMON said, 'If one were walking by the way and studying and interrupted his study saying, "How fine is this tree!" or, "How fine is this newly ploughed field!", Scripture regards him as if he were guilty against his own soul.'

Sayings of the Fathers

IF YOU study the laws about sacrifice, that is to me as if you had offered them.

Pesikta Kahana

TEACHING

YUDA NESIAH sent Rabbi Hiyya, Rabbi Assi and Rabbi Ammi to traverse the cities in the land of Israel in order to appoint Bible and Mishnah teachers. They came to a city, and they found no teacher of Bible or Mishnah. They said: 'Bring to us the guardians of the city.' So they brought to them the senators of the town. They said: 'Are these the guardians of the town? They are the destroyers of the town.' 'Who then', they asked, 'are the guardians of the town?' They said: 'The teachers of Bible and Mishnah', as it is said, 'Unless the Lord guard the city, the watchman wakes but in vain.' (*Psalm 127:1*)

Talmud

LEVI YITSHAK of Berdichev used to say: Do not despair if you preach and see no result. You can be sure that the seed you have planted will blossom in the heart of one listener.

PINCHAS OF KORETZ

WISDOM

DO NOT consider a thing as proof just because you find it written in books. Just as a liar will deceive with his tongue, he will not be deterred from doing the same thing with his pen. They are total fools who accept a thing as convincing proof just because it is in writing.

MOSES MAIMONIDES

TRUTH IS the seal of God.

Talmud

THERE ARE four characteristic traits among those who sit in the presence of the wise: a sponge, a funnel, a strainer, and a sieve. A sponge – which absorbs everything. A funnel – that lets in at one end and discharges at the other. A strainer – which lets out the wine and retains the dregs. A sieve – which lets the coarse flour pass out and retains the fine flour.

Sayings of the Fathers

BEN ZOMA said, 'Who is wise? He who learns from all men, as it is said, "From all my teachers have I acquired understanding." '

Sayings of the Fathers

THERE IS gold, and a multitude of rubies: but the lips of knowledge are a precious jewel.

Proverbs 20:15

THE PROPER study of a wise man is not how to die, but how to live.

BENEDICT SPINOZA

EVEN A fool, when he holdeth his peace, is counted wise: and he that shutteth his lips is esteemed a man of understanding.

Proverbs 17:28

THERE ARE seven characteristics of an uncultured person, and seven of a wise man. A wise man does not speak before one who is superior to him in wisdom. He does not break in upon the words of his fellow. He is not hasty to answer. He questions in accordance with the subject matter, and answers to the point. He speaks upon the first thing first, and the last thing last. Regarding what he has not heard, he says, 'I do not understand it.' And he admits the truth. The reverse of (all) these is characteristic of an uncultured man.

Sayings of the Fathers

GIVE INSTRUCTION to a wise man, and he will yet be wiser: teach a just man, and he will increase in learning.

Proverbs 9:9

DO NOT struggle vaingloriously for the small triumph of showing yourself in the right and a wise person in the wrong. You are not one bit the wiser as a result.

ASHER BEN YEHIEL

JOSE BEN Joezer of Zeredah and Jose ben Jochanan of Jerusalem received (the tradition) from them. Jose ben Joezer said, 'Let your house be a meeting-house for the wise, and sit amidst the dust of their feet, and drink in their words with thirst.'

Sayings of the Fathers

HATRED

ENEMIES

REJOICE NOT when thine enemy falleth, and let not thine heart be glad when he stumbleth.

Proverbs 24:17

IF THINE enemy be hungry, give him bread to eat; and if he be thirsty, give him water to drink.

Proverbs 25:21

I AM like a gentleman among barbarians,
Like a lion among a colony of parrots and monkeys.

MOSES BEN EZRA

WHOEVER TAKES vengeance or bears a grudge acts like one who, having cut one hand while handling a knife, avenges himself by stabbing the other hand.

Talmud

If others speak ill of you, let the worst they say seem to you small. If you speak ill of others, let a small thing seem to you big until you go to appease the person of whom you have spoken.

Derek Erez Zuta

Dare not to rejoice when your enemy comes to the ground, but give him food when he hungers.

Eliezer ben Isaac

Do not misuse your power against anyone. Who can tell whether you will some day be powerless yourself.

Asher ben Yehiel

He used to say, 'Despise no man, nor discard any thing, for there is no man who does not have his hour, and there is nothing which does not have its place.'

Sayings of the Fathers

WRATH

RABBI SIMON ben Elazar said, 'Do not placate your fellow man in the hour of his wrath.'

Sayings of the Fathers

ANIMOSITY

THOU SHALT not hate thy brother in thine heart.

Leviticus 19:17

WHEN THE Egyptian hosts were drowning in the Red Sea, the angels in heaven were about to break forth in songs of jubilation. But the Holy One, blessed be he, silenced them with the words: 'My creatures are perishing, and yet you are ready to sing!'

Talmud

SOME INDIVIDUALS make vows because of hatred of others, swearing, for example, that they will not let this or that person sit at the same table with them or come under the same roof. Such people should seek the mercy of God so that they will find some cure for the diseases of their soul.

PHILO

IF A man dislikes his wife, he should not pray that God give him another wife. Rather, if she annoys him or is displeasing to him, he should pray that God will turn her heart to love him and find favour in his eyes, so that they will renew their love for one another … If one has an enemy, he should pray to the Holy One, not to to slay or punish his enemy, but rather to help them both bring about peace.

Sefer Hasidim

HATRED STIRRETH up strifes: but love covereth all sins.

Proverbs 10:12

HE THAT is soon angry dealeth foolishly.

Proverbs 14:17

IF FOLK knew what others intended for them, they would kill themselves.

Yiddish Proverb

ANGER

BE NOT ready to quarrel.

ASHER BEN YEHIEL

IT IS certain that the ininquities of the angry person outweigh his merits.

Talmud

A SOFT answer turneth away wrath: but grievous words stir up anger.

Proverbs 15:1

THE ANGRY man forgets what he has learnt, becoming increasingly stupid.

Talmud

MAN'S ANGER controls him, but God controls his anger. He is master of his wrath. Man's jealousy controls him, but God controls his jealousy.

Midrash Psalms

ANGER DEPRIVES a wise person of his wisdom, and a prophet of his vision.

Talmud

RABBI MENACHEM Mendel of Lubavitch used to restrain an angry outburst until he had looked in the codes to discover whether anger is permissible in that particular instance. But how much genuine anger could he feel after searching for the authority in the code of Jewish Law?

Hasidic Tale

PRAYER

WORSHIP

RABBI JUDAH ben Shalom said: 'If a poor man comes, and pleads before another, that person does not listen to him. If a rich man comes, he listens to, and receives him at once. God does not act this way. All are equal before him: women, slaves, rich and poor.'

Exodus Rabbah

TO AN earthly king, if a poor man greets him, or one who has a burn on his hand, it is a disgrace. In such a case the king does not reply. But God is not like this. Everybody is acceptable to him. He says: 'Praise me, and it is acceptable to me.'

Midrash Psalms

RABBI JOHANAN said: 'What is the service of God? Prayer.'

Midrash Psalms

GOD SAYS to Israel: 'I asked you to pray in the synagogue in your city. But if you cannot pray there, pray in your field. And if you cannot pray there, pray in bed. And if you cannot pray there, then meditate in your heart and be still.'

Pesikta Kahana

THE CONGREGATION of Israel says: 'We are poor. We have no sacrifices to bring as a sin offering.' God replies: 'I need only words.'

Exodus Rabbah

WHY IS the prayer of the righteous like a rake? As the rake turns the grain from place to place, so the prayer of the righteous turns the attributes of God from the attribute of wrath to the attribute of mercy.

Talmud

'TO SERVE the Lord your God with all your heart' (*Deuteronomy 11:13*). What is a service of the heart? It is prayer.

Sifre Deuteronomy

RABBI ELAZAR would first give a coin to a poor man, and then pray.

Talmud

LEVI BEN Sisi fasted and prayed for rain in vain. He said: 'Master of the world! You have gone up and taken your seat in heaven, and show no consideration for your children.' Rain fell, but Levi became lame. Rabbi Elazar said: 'One must never reproach God.'

Talmud

SOME PEOPLE think of business when they are in the synagogue. Is it too much to ask them to think of God when they are at business?

NAHMAN OF KOSOV

PRAYER SHOULD not be recited as if a man were reading a document.

Talmud

RABBI SAFRA used to pray: 'May it be your will, O Lord our God, to grant peace in the household above and the household below, among the students who occupy themselves with your Torah, whether they devote themselves to it for its own sake, or not. As for those who devote themselves to it not for its own sake, may it be your will that they shall (at last) devote themselves to it for its own sake.

Talmud

THE BAAL Shem Tov used to say: Do not laugh at a man who gestures as he prays fervently. He gestures in order to keep himself from distracting thoughts which intrude upon him and threaten to drown his prayer. You would not laugh at a drowning man who gestures in the water in order to save himself.

AARON OF APT

EVEN AN iron wall cannot separate God from a Jew who is praying.

Talmud

INTENTION

RABBI NEHEMIAH said: 'If a man intends to commit a sin, God does not reckon it to him until he has done it. But if he intends to fulfil a commandment, then although he had not opportunity to do it, God writes it down to him immediately as if he had done it.'

Midrash Psalms

RABBI HIYYA ben Abba said in the name of Rabbi Johanan: 'Whoever prolongs his prayer, and calculates on it, will eventually come to pain of heart.'

Talmud

RAB SAID: He whose mind is not quieted should not pray.

Talmud

RABBI SAMUEL ben Nahmani said: If you have directed your heart in prayer, be assured that your prayer will be heard by God.

Midrash Psalms

SIMON THE Pious said: 'In his prayer a man should think that the *Shekhinah* is before him.'

Talmud

HOW LONG must a man persist in prayer? Rabbi Judah said: 'Till his heart faints, as it says. "A prayer of an afflicted one when he faints."'

Midrash Psalms

RABBI ELAZAR said: 'Always let a man test himself: if he can direct his heart, let him pray. If he cannot, he should not pray.'

Talmud

RABBI AMMI said: 'Man's prayer is not accepted unless he puts his heart in his hands.'

Talmud

A MAN must purify his heart before he prays.

Exodus Rabbah

IT MATTERS not whether you do much or little, as long as your heart is directed to heaven

Talmud

RABBI JOHANAN said: 'He who recites the praise of God more than is fitting will be torn away from the world.'

Talmud

RABBI SAMUEL ben Nahmani said: If you have directed your heart in prayer, be assured that your prayer will be heard by God.

Midrash Psalms

PRAISE

THIS IS the day which the Lord has made; we will rejoice and be glad in it.

Psalm 118:24

THE PRAYER of a shepherd who 'did not know how to pray': Lord of the universe! It is apparent and known to you, that if you had cattle and gave them to me to tend, though I take wages for tending from all others, from you I would take nothing, because I love you.

Sefer Hasidim

THE LORD reigneth, he is clothed with majesty; the Lord is clothed with strength, wherewith he hath girded himself: the world also is established, that it cannot be moved. Thy throne is established of old: thou art from everlasting.

Psalm 93:1–3

SWEET HYMNS and songs will I indite
To sing of thee by day and night
Of thee, who art my soul's delight

How doth my soul within me yearn
Beneath thy shadow to return
Thy secret mysteries to learn!

And even while yet thy glory fires
My words, and hymns of praise inspires,
Thy love it is my heart desires.

Thy glory shall my discourse be;
In images picture thee,
Although thyself I cannot see

O thou whose word is truth alway,
Thy people seek thy face this day;
O be thou near them when they pray.

O may my words of blessing rise
To thee, who, throned above the skies,
Art just and mighty, great and wise.

חג המצות
להדליק נר של יום טוב
פסח
והגדת לבנך ביום ההוא

My meditation day and night,
May it be pleasant in thy sight,
For thou art all my soul's delight.

JUDAH THE PIOUS

A PERSON is obligated to bless God for the evil that befalls him just as he blesses him for the good.

Talmud

A GROUP of Slonim Hasidim, who were caught in the 'selection' stood together, preparing themselves for the moment of *Kiddush Hashem* (the sanctification of the Divine Name) in death. In the midst of the group stood the *dayyan*, Rabbi Nissan, who called to the others: 'Jews! Let us not forget that today is *Purim*. Let us drink '*L'hayyim*, to life.' He poured out a cupful and said again: '*L'hayyim*!' He got hold of a few other Jews and started dancing. His face was shining as he sang the traditional *Purim* song, *Shoshanat Ya'akov* and he shouted with joy until a German bullet silenced him.

ELIEZER BERKOVITS

WE GIVE thanks unto thee, for thou art the Lord our God and the God of our fathers for ever and ever; thou art the Rock of our lives, the shield of our salvation through every generation.

Prayerbook

PRAISE YE the Lord, O give thanks unto the Lord; for he is good: for his mercy endureth for ever.

Psalm 106:1

O GIVE thanks unto the Lord; call upon his name: make known his deeds among the people. Sing unto him, sing psalms unto him: talk ye of all his wondrous works. Glory ye in his holy name: let the heart of them rejoice that seek the Lord.

Psalm 105:1–3

O SING unto the Lord a new song: sing unto the Lord, all the earth. Sing unto the Lord, bless his name; shew forth his salvation from day to day. Declare his glory among the heathen, his wonders among all people. For the Lord is great, and greatly to be praised; he is to be feared above all gods. For all the gods of the nations are idols: but the Lord made the heavens. Honour and majesty are before him: strength and beauty are in his sanctuary.

Psalm 96:1–6

LORD, THOU hast been our dwelling place in all generations. Before the mountains were brought forth, or ever thou hadst formed the earth and the world, even from everlasting to everlasting, thou art God.

Psalm 90:1–2

THE LORD is my light and my salvation; whom shall I fear? the Lord is the strength of my life; of whom shall I be afraid? When the wicked, even mine enemies and my foes, came upon me to eat up my flesh, they stumbled and fell.

Psalm 27:1–2

I WILL sing of the mercies of the Lord for ever: with my mouth will I make known thy faithfulness to all generations.

Psalm 89:1

CLAP YOUR hands, all ye people; shout unto God with the voice of triumph. For the Lord most high is terrible; he is a great king over all the earth. He shall subdue the people under us, and the nations under our feet.

Psalm 47:1–3

AS THE hart panteth after the water brooks, so panteth my soul after thee, O God. My soul thirsteth for God, for the living God.

Psalm 42:1–2

REJOICE IN the Lord, O ye righteous: for praise is comely for the upright. Praise the Lord with harp: sing unto him with the psaltery and an instrument of ten strings. Sing unto him a new song; play skilfully with a loud noise.

Psalm 33:1–3

THE HEAVENS declare the glory of God; and the firmament sheweth his handiwork.

Psalm 19:1

I WILL praise thee, O Lord, with my whole heart; I will shew forth all thy marvellous works. I will be glad and rejoice in thee: I will sing praise to thy name, O thou most high.

Psalm 9:1–2

SUPPLICATION

O LORD, God of my salvation, I have cried day and night before thee: Let my prayer come before thee: incline thine ear unto my cry; For my soul is full of troubles: and my life draweth nigh unto the grave.

Psalm 88:1–3

RABBI ELIEZER said: If a man makes his prayer a fixed task, his prayer is no supplication.

Talmud

MAY IT be thy will, O Lord our God and God of our fathers, to make us familiar with thy law, and to make us cleave to thy commandments. O lead us not into sin, or transgression, iniquity, temptation or shame.

Talmud

BLESSED ART thou, O Lord our God, king of the universe, who makest the bands of sleep to fall upon mine eyes, and slumber upon mine eyelids. May it be thy will, O Lord my God and God of my fathers, to suffer me to lie down in peace and to let me rise up again in peace. Let not my thoughts trouble me, nor evil dreams, nor evil fancies, but let my rest be perfect before thee.

Talmud

SOVEREIGN OF all worlds! Not because of our righteous acts do we lay our supplications before thee, but because of thine abundant mercies. What are we? What is our life? What is our piety? What our righteousness? What our helpfulness? What our strength? What our might? What shall we say before thee, O Lord our God and God of our fathers? Are not all the mighty men as nought before thee, the men of renown as though they had not been, the wise as if without knowledge, and the men of understanding as if without discernment?

Prayerbook

GRANT PEACE, welfare, blessing, grace, loving-kindness and mercy unto us and unto all Israel, thy people. Bless us, O our father, even all of us together, with the light of thy countenance; for by the light of thy countenance thou hast given us, O Lord our God, the law of life, loving-kindness and righteousness, blessing, mercy, life and peace; and may it be good in thy sight to bless thy people Israel at all times and in every hour with thy peace.

Prayerbook

GIVE US understanding, O Lord our God, to know thy ways; open our hearts to fear thee, and forgive us so that we may be redeemed. Keep us far from sorrow; satiate us on the pastures of thy land, and gather our scattered ones from the four corners of the earth. Let them that go astray be judged according to thy will, and wave thy hand over the wicked. Let the righteous rejoice in the rebuilding of thy city, and in the establishment of thy temple, and in the flourishing of the horn of David thy servant, and in the clear-shining light of the son of Jesse, thine anointed. Even before we call, do thou answer.

Prayerbook

LOOK, WE beseech thee, and speedily have mercy upon thy people for thy name's sake in thine abundant mercies. O Lord our God, spare and be merciful: save the sheep of thy pasture; let not wrath rule over us, for our eyes are bent upon thee; save us for thy name's sake. Have mercy upon us for the sake of thy covenant; look and answer us in time of trouble, for salvation is thine, O Lord.

Prayerbook

SOUND THE great horn for our freedom; lift up the banner to gather our exiles, and gather us from the four corners of the earth.

Prayerbook

HEAL US, O Lord, and we shall be healed; save us and we shall be saved; for thou art our praise. Grant a perfect healing to all our wounds, for thou, almighty king, art a faithful and merciful physician.

Prayerbook

GIVE US understanding, O Lord our God, to know thy ways; circumcise our hearts to fear thee, and forgive us so that we may be redeemed.

Talmud

HEAR ME when I call, O God of my righteousness: thou hast enlarged me when I was in distress; have mercy upon me, and hear my prayer.

Psalm 4:1–2

GIVE EAR to my words, O Lord, consider my meditation. Hearken unto the voice of my cry, my king, and my God: for unto thee will I pray.

Psalm 5:1–2

O LORD, rebuke me not in thine anger, neither chasten me in thy hot displeasure. Have mercy upon me, O Lord; for I am weak; O Lord heal me; for my bones are vexed.

Psalm 6:1–2

DEATH AND BEYOND

DEATH

NAKED CAME I out of my mother's womb, and naked shall I return thither: the Lord gave, and the Lord hath taken away; blessed be the name of the Lord.

Job 1:20

ALL GO unto one place; all are of the dust, and all turn to dust again.

Ecclesiastes 3:20

RABBI ELIEZER said, 'Repent one day before your death.' His disciples asked: 'Does a person know on what day he is going to die?' 'All the more reason to repent today, lest one die tomorrow', he replied. 'In this manner, one's whole life will be spent in repentance.'

Talmud

A PERSON cannot say to the Angel of Death: 'Wait till I settle my accounts.'

Ecclesiastes Rabbah

AS THE womb takes in and gives forth again, so the grave takes in and will give forth again.

Talmud

EVERY MAN knows that he must die, but no one believes it.

Yiddish Proverb

SHROUDS HAVE no pockets.

Yiddish Proverb

THE CONTEMPLATION of death should place within the soul elevation and peace. Above all, it should make us see things in their true light.

C. G. MONTEFIORE

WHEN RABBI Bunam was lying on his deathbed, he said to his wife who was weeping bitterly: 'Why do you weep? All my life has been given to me merely so that I might learn to die.'

Hasidic Tale

HEREAFTER

THERE ARE those who gain eternity in a lifetime, others who gain it in one short hour.

Talmud

WHEN RABBI Akiva was taken out to be executed, it was time for the recital of the *Shema*, and while they tore at his flesh with iron combs, he was accepting upon himself the Kingdom of Heaven … He drew out the word *echad* (one) until he died while saying it. A voice from heaven went forth and proclaimed: 'Happy are you Akiva, that you are destined for the life of the World-to-Come.'

Talmud

BEFORE HIS death, Rabbi Zusya said: 'In the coming world, they will not ask me: "Why were you not Moses?" They will ask me: "Why were you not Zusya?"

Hasidic Tale

RABBI JOHANAN said: 'The Jerusalem of the World to Come is unlike the Jerusalem of this world. All can enter the Jerusalem of this world. But only those who are appointed for it will enter the Jerusalem of the World-to-Come.'

Talmud

FOUR SHALL not enter Paradise: the scoffer, the liar, the hypocrite, and the slanderer.

Talmud

GOD, THE source of life, has placed in our nature the blessed hope of immortality, by which we may console ourselves for the vanity of life, and overcome the dread of death.

YEDAYA PENINA

RABBI JACOB said, 'The world is like a vestibule to the World-to-Come; prepare yourself in the vestibule that you may enter into the hall.'

Sayings of the Fathers

IN THE World-to-Come, there will be no eating, nor drinking, nor procreation, nor business, nor jealousy, nor hatred, nor competition. But the righteous will sit with crowns on their heads, feasting on the radiance of the *Shekinah*, the Divine Presence.

Talmud

HE USED to say, 'Better is one hour of repentance and good actions in this world than the whole life of the World-to-Come. But better is one hour of bliss of spirit in the world to come than all the life of this world.'

Sayings of the Fathers

BOOK OF LIFE

'TO BE inscribed in the Book of Life.' This must be understood in a spiritual sense. When a man clings to the love of God, and, putting his trust in his infinite mercy, takes upon himself the yoke of the Kingdom of heaven – he therewith inscribes himself in the Book of Life. Whereas the man, a slave to his passions, who so loses his belief in the all-embracing love of God that he fails to repent and return to his father in heaven, this despairing of the love of God is equivalent to his being inscribed – God forbid – in the Book of Death.

BAAL SHEM TOV

PROVIDENCE

IF A man is in distress, let him not call on (the angels) Michael or Gabriel, but let him call me directly. I will hearken to him straightaway.

Talmud

NO PERSON bruises his finger here on earth unless it was decreed against him in heaven.

Talmud

A RABBI was once passing through a field where he saw a very old man planting an oak tree. 'Why are you planting that tree?' he said. 'Surely you do not expect to live long enough to see the acorn turning into an oak tree?' 'Ah,' replied the old man, 'my ancestors planted trees not for themselves, but for us so that we might enjoy their shade and fruit. I am doing the same for those who will come after me.'

Mishnah

BE STRONG and of good courage; be not afraid, neither be thou dismayed: for the Lord thy God is with thee withersoever thou goest.

Joshua 1:9

NOTHING HAPPENS to a person except by the decree of the Holy One, blessed be he.

Sefer Hasidim

DO NOT say: 'Tomorrow I will make provision.' For the day has ended, and you do not know what the next day may bring.

BAHYA IBN PAKUDA

A MAN has a protector. If he worries him too much, the protector says, 'I will forget him since he worries me.' But God is not like this. However much you worry him, he will receive you.

Talmud

KINGDOM OF GOD

THE KINGDOM of God – the rabbis held – is inconsistent with a state of social misery. They were not satisfied with feeding the poor. Their great ideal was not to allow a man to be poor, not to allow him to come down into the depths of poverty. They say, 'Try to prevent it by teaching him a trade. Try all methods before you permit him to become an object of charity, which must degrade him.'

SOLOMON SCHECHTER

DO NOT seek for the City of God on earth, for it is not built of wood or stone; but seek it in the soul of the man who is at peace with himself.

PHILO

HOLY SPIRIT

THE HOLY Spirit rests only on the person who has a joyous heart.

Talmud

THE SOUL

As God fills the world, so the soul fills the body. As God sees, but is not seen, so the soul sees but is not itself seen. As God feeds the whole world, so the soul feeds the entire body. As God is pure, so the soul is pure. As God dwells in the innermost precincts (of the Temple), so the soul dwells in the innermost part of the body.

Talmud

My God, the soul which you have given me is pure, for you created it. You formed it and made it live within me. You watch over it, but one day you will take it from me to everlasting life.

Jewish Prayer Book

INDEX OF SOURCES

ACKNOWLEDGEMENTS

The publisher would like to thank the following institutions for assistance and permission to produce the following pictures:

Robert Harding Picture Library (pp. 65, 73, 77, 137, 141, 165, 172, 216, 240); The Hutchison Library (pp. 44, 53, 61, 121, 133, 152, 205, 224, 228, 249); Sonia Halliday Photographs (pp. 69, 85, 145, 181, 220, 244).